grow up gay

growing up gay

New Zealand men tell their stories

James Allan

GODWIT

I'd like to express my gratitude to Warwick Roger, who made me a writer; to my partner Kim, whose unwavering love and respect is the absolute centre of my life; to my mother, who has always followed the golden rule, 'If you can't say anything nice, don't say anything at all'; to Jock Phillips, Chief Historian, and Megan Hutching, Oral Historian, at the Historical Branch, Department of Internal Affairs, for their outstanding support of this project.

I am donating my share from the sales of this book, 10 per cent of the retail price, to the Bruce Burnett Fund, The Gay and Lesbian Community Centre, Herne Bay House and Ice Breakers/Rainbow Youth. This book is very much a gay community effort and our community should benefit from the generosity and honesty of the men who have shared their stories with us.

First published 1996 by

Godwit Publishing Ltd
15 Rawene Road, P.O. Box 34-683
Birkenhead, Auckland, New Zealand

© 1996 James Allen

ISBN 0 908877 84 6

Text and cover design by Christine Hansen
Production and typesetting by Kate Greenaway
Photograph of James Allan by Sean Shadbolt
Printed in New Zealand

Contents

This book is dedicated to a small circle of friends:

John Pound, 1950-1986.
Died of an AIDS-related illness.

Richard Davies, 1952-1986.
Died of an AIDS-related illness.

Ross Kennedy, 1947-1987.
Died of an AIDS-related illness.

Steve Wright, 1954-1989.
Died of an AIDS-related illness.

Michael Bunyard, 1952-1993.
Died of an AIDS-related illness.

Lindsay Ridge, 1951-1994.
Died of an AIDS-related illness.

Preface

Inspired by collections of gay men's life histories from Germany, America, England and Australia, I started assembling this collection of New Zealand gay men's life histories in 1993.

I started by contacting 12 gay men I hoped might let me record their life histories. Because being gay is still, despite recent legal and social changes, a surprisingly stigmatised sexual orientation, I approached only gay men who were already openly gay and in the public eye. From the outset I made it clear that they had complete control over their stories.

I asked each man to tell me his life history, concentrating on those episodes he thought most relevant to his development as a gay male. Each man ran his own session — I simply sat and scribbled down their words. Some interviews were a light and breezy one-hour chat; others an intense, emotionally exhausting, three-hour confession.

I drafted my notes into chronological life histories and returned these edited stories to their owners for comment and alteration. Only four returned their stories, re-edited and cleared for publication. I gave the others about six months to get back to me before I contacted them. I didn't want anyone to feel badgered into taking part. When I did contact the final eight, they all said they'd decided to withdraw from the project because either they'd changed so much since their interview they didn't recognise themselves in their stories, or seeing their biography written down came as a real shock, and they couldn't face the idea of their stories being public knowledge. These desertions upset me. All eight stories were wonderful, and I'd put a lot of work into them. But, in the non-manipulative spirit in which I'd started my project, I simply thanked everyone, and wished them goodbye and good luck.

Down and slightly out, I began to doubt the value and viability of this project. Seeking outside confirmation of its worth, I approached the Historical Branch, Department of Internal Affairs, for an Oral History grant which would allow me to interview gay men around the country. I was strongly encouraged when the Historical Branch's Australian Sesquicentennial Gift Trust for Oral History Committee awarded me $3000 to complete my project.

Revived in spirit and eager to attract new interview subjects, I promoted the project on gay radio programmes and in New Zealand's two national gay publications, *Out* and *Man To Man*, asking for interested participants to contact me. Eventually another 13 gay men lined up to be interviewed. Eight contacted me. The others were suggested to me and I contacted them.

I had hoped for around 40 starters, and attribute the lack of response to two reasons. Firstly, gay men are still surprisingly wary about coming out publicly. Secondly, most people are essentially modest and don't consider their lives noteworthy enough to be recorded. All the men whose life histories I did record insisted no one would find them interesting.

This time around I left a six-month gap between the first and final interview. This breathing space was essential for people to have the time to evaluate their life histories and get used to the idea of them being made public. Every day I see people railroaded into interviews, and I appreciate the subsequent feelings of violation and anger they have when they feel used, chewed up and spat out by a rapacious journalist. I wanted this to be a collaborative effort, one that everyone would be pleased and proud to be part of.

Of the 13 men I interviewed, only five withdrew. Once again, although their decision to withdraw upset me, I did not badger anyone to stay with the project. I wanted the men who took part in it to be totally supportive of the stories being published using their real names. And they are. Only two have decided to shelter under the umbrella of anonymity, and one has done so not for his own sake but to protect his children from being teased at school.

The stories are, apart from my minimal editing and chronological ordering, all their own work. What fascinated me was how the stories changed throughout the editing process. What someone considered a pivotal point in their life when they first told me their story in May was edited out in December as being not particularly relevant. Obviously we're constantly editing our past as we live in the present. Everyone's story went through about four major edits and rewrites before we ended up with a satisfactory final version.

As I said, I left the story-telling very much in the hands of the autobiographers. At the final stage of preparation for publication, a Wellington editor, Jane Parkin, stepped in and evaluated and re-edited the life histories, deleting here, asking for clarification there. Jane did a tremendous job, and all the guys approved her work and happily co-operated with her alterations. She really focused the stories, getting rid of repetitions and digressions.

We now have an excellent collection of the life histories of 12 gay New Zealand men. Apart from Chris Carter and Mika, most of us are unknown, ordinary guys, which makes this collection all the more valuable. There's a lot of media focus on famous gay men, but not that much recognition given to the everyday gay bloke.

The constant motivation for everyone involved with this project was to spare other young gay men the confusion, loneliness and torment we suffered growing up gay. We all want them to know there's a place for them in Aotearoa and that anyone, not just the rich man, the rock star and the designer, but also the teacher, the plumber and the engineer, can live open, happy, successful gay lives.

James S. Allan, 1995

Introduction

Think of this book as a portable encounter group committed to strengthening the gay community.

Encounter groups, where gay men meet and talk about their lives, have proved highly effective in building self-esteem and a personal sense of power. Through these discussions gay men develop a sense of community. Young men learn they're not alone; that others before them have gone through the turmoil of coming out and growing up gay. Older gay men share past experiences and compare notes on growing grey and gay in a youth-oriented world. Everybody realises that others, too, are grappling with problems of love, intimacy and sexuality.

The men who appear in this book, sharing the most intimate details of their lives, were motivated by a desire to educate and empower others in the gay community, particularly the young, the isolated, the distressed. Since the wider community refuses to recognise, educate and support gay youth, the gay community must reach out to them.

The almost total absence of gay people in public life means young men growing into the knowledge of their sexuality have very little information about the gay community. Their future appears to hold little promise. They hear their sexual orientation discussed as an illness, an aberration, a social problem. The most prevalent images of homosexuality they receive are the negative, often cruel stereotypes arising from ignorance and bigotry. They hear powerful politicians say gays are sick and perverted child molesters. They hear respected churchmen say gays aren't good enough to be priests or teachers.

Society tells them that to be gay is to be wrong. Growing up in a world that paints such a bleak picture of their future prospects, it's little wonder the suicide rate among gay youth is tragically high. Lacking gay family members and role models, most gay youth consider themselves an alien presence in their family circle. They know gays aren't welcome. Fear of rejection makes even discussing their sexuality an overwhelming hurdle.

Why is the general population prejudiced against gays? For the same reason they've shown prejudice, at various times, against Jews, Asians, Polynesians — a fear of the unknown. A fear of strangers is a basic protective human/animal response. It keeps baby apes out of the clutches of predators and makes baby humans cry when a stranger picks them up. Clustered together in our tribal groups, humans reject outsiders as dangerous, potentially divisive interlopers.

This insider/outsider business makes growing up gay a peculiarly difficult experience. We start life as insiders, only realising our outsider status as the years go by. Happy children become unhappy gay adolescents. Growing up gay is a difficult, solitary, secretive act that takes place in full public view.

Gay men the world over live similar lives and dream similar dreams. The poet W. H. Auden invented a word for this international homo-culture, 'homintern', meaning the life experiences and innate personality traits that connect gays more closely with gays from other countries than with the heterosexual citizens of their own country, or even their own family. I know I often feel closer to a gay foreigner I've known for five minutes than to heterosexual relations I've known all my life.

Around the world growing up gay means having to find a place for yourself within an unwelcoming community. Gay men are forced to question and evaluate the accepted rules of society, discarding the unworthy and honouring the good. The ancient Greeks considered a truly civilised man to be one who had deeply considered the world, his society and his place in it. Every gay man does this as he grows up in a society in which he doesn't quite fit.

Through harsh experience, gay men learn who we are and what society is. Unlike those heterosexual sleepwalkers who stroll through life without ever questioning the status quo, gay men are highly aware of the place of the individual within society, and of the bonds of duty and respect that bind any civilised community together. We civilise ourselves. The question now is, 'Who's going to civilise the heterosexuals?'

James Allan

I was born on Black Friday, June 1952, in Hamilton, in the Waikato. My mother, Marie, was aged 30. My father, John, was 31. My brother, Jack, was four. My parents had six more children, two boys and four girls, over the next 12 years.

My parents had a mixed marriage. On her bedside table my mother had a leather-bound, three-volume edition of Alexander Sholokov's *Quiet Flows the Don*. My father's bedside reading was *Best Bets*, *Truth* and war comic books.

My parents met during World War Two, when my mother, an Otaki lawyer's daughter who had attended Wellington's elegant Sacré Coeur Convent boarding school, travelled north to work as a pharmacist in Hamilton Hospital. She rented a room in my grandmother-to-be's rooming house, where she met my father. He had grown up on his family's small farm at Te Kowhai, a village a few kilometres west of Hamilton.

It's easy to see why she fell in love with him. Dad was a very magnetic, larger-than-life personality. Tall, beefy, strong in body and temperament, he was keen on rugby, racing and beer — a perfect character for the times. In Mum, Dad found a supportive, attractive, clever woman with a good head for business, who stood by him and helped his every endeavour. I never heard them fight. He always called her 'Dear'.

They were successful in every business they took on. When they first married, Mum joined Dad working a milk run. Next they bought a milkbar. When I was aged four — my first memory is sitting in the cab of the moving van — we left Hamilton for Puhoi, a tiny settlement one hour's drive north of Auckland, where Mum and Dad leased the Puhoi Hotel.

In those days Puhoi township consisted of the hotel, a general store, a hall, a church and a convent. We were the only kids in town. The others lived on farms. My first teachers, the nuns, dressed in heavy woollen brown habits with big wooden rosary beads looped around wide leather belts. They were tough and would smack you on the knuckles with a ruler if you were naughty.

My first day at school I got smacked for wetting my pants. It happened during story time and I was too shy to interrupt and ask where the toilet was. My brother was hauled in from the big kids' room to clean up my mess. I also wet my pants during Mass one Sunday morning, and fled the church in great confusion. I must have been a very nervy child. I was sent home once for having bright red hives all over my arms and legs. Later on, at age 10, I developed the nervous skin complaint shingles: big watery blisters came up all over one side of my torso.

Puhoi was isolated, old-fashioned and self-sufficient. We had electricity, but the hotel's cooking and water heating was done on a big wood-burning range that blazed day and night. We had our own wood shed and hen run, and our milk came in billies, fresh from the farm.

This was a time when men were men — they'd all been

through the war, fighting to preserve their way of life — and women were women, supposed to stay home, bear children and help their husbands make a go of it. Children, a good source of unpaid labour, were expected to help their parents make a go of it too. For us kids this meant being woken up by my father every morning at 6.30. Our first job was to load a tray with cups, saucers, a couple of big pots of tea and packets of Griffin's Round Wine biscuits. We'd go around the guests' bedrooms, waking them up with a cup of tea and biscuits. I know I'd make a great air hostie. I've been asking, 'Tea? Milk? Sugar?' practically since I could walk.

Early morning tea done, we moved on to the bar, which reeked of stale cigarettes and beer. We would vacuum the carpet, re-stock the fridges and the cigarette dispensers, wash the glasses, clean the hand basins and mop the toilets. Picking soggy cigarette butts out of the urinals at 7 a.m. was not a favourite task. To this day, I loathe the smell of beer and have never drunk it.

During weekends and school holidays we'd have extra chores to do, like helping wait the breakfast tables, doing the dishes, sweeping the beer garden and filling beer flagons before being allowed 'out'. These jobs seemed to last for ever. Nana — Mum's mother — said we gave the impression we hated our father because we'd run away whenever he appeared. It wasn't Dad we were scared of — we were frightened he'd have a job for us to do!

What I did hate was the way he'd wake us up. He'd pull the blankets right off the bed, exposing us totally. We'd snuggle down into whatever warmth was left in the mattress, clinging to sleep for as long as possible — if we hadn't wet the bed, that is. We were chronic bed wetters, and had to sleep with crinkly, cold plastic sheets under the cotton ones.

The older I get, the more I realise what a strange circle life is, and how we turn into our parents. Now the sight of kids lying about makes me keen to find them something to do. And I get Kim out of bed by pulling the blankets off him exactly the same way Dad used to pull them off us.

It would have been hard to find a childhood more isolated from outside influences than ours. There was no television. The nearest picture theatre — the flicks — was in Warkworth, a long drive away. The radio was our link to the outside world, but there weren't any pop music stations.

Homosexuality didn't exist. There were no gay heroes or villains, no gay role models, not even the word gay. Yet it was in this isolated environment that my gay sensibility first showed itself, which proves to me the truth that we're born gay, with an inherent gay sensibility that informs everything we do. We don't learn to be queer — we just are.

I always loved fantasy, and my fantasies were always *femme*. I never dreamed about being an All Black. Whenever Mum caught the bus to Auckland, to do the banking, I'd ask for a dolly's tea set so I could play tea parties. I loved reading, especially books where people were magically transformed, and dressing up — I'm haunted by a photo of me dressed in one of Mum's frocks, pushing a pram around the back yard.

I must've been aged around eight when I pinned a picture of a beautiful woman, some glamorous screen goddess, to the wall above my bed. I cut the picture out of a *Pix* or *Post* — popular Australian tabloid magazines. My goddess had tousled dark curls, bright red lips and big golden earrings. She peered at the camera in a very sultry fashion, over one shoulder. In every one of the summer holiday snaps taken that year, I'm posing just like her, peering at the camera over my shoulder. To add to the queer glory of the photos,

I'm wearing my favourite shirt, a bright red satin number Mum made for my role as a pirate in a school play. In a time of dull conformity, when every Kiwi kid wore grey shorts and T-shirts, I certainly stood out.

Another early gay marker was my dancing. I would dance the hula for hotel guests. Imagine this little boy wiggling his hips and waving his hands in an undulating, very feminine manner. I must have been a bizarre sight. I have no idea where I learned about the hula or even why I wanted to dance it. God knows how my big, butch father coped with the looks his beery mates must have given this pint-sized female impersonator. How come I, aged five or six, was channelling the spirit of a Kings Cross drag queen? Nothing in my immediate environment introduced or encouraged these queer displays. Nature over nurture is the obvious answer.

For years, these memories of my *femme* behaviour had me cringing with embarrassment. Recently, though, I've rid myself of my internalised hatred for being a boy possessing feminine traits. Why should I feel guilt and self-loathing about innocent behaviour that came naturally to me? It's been quite an effort, but I've managed to appreciate the sweet side of these memories. These days I wonder if I acted *femme* because we only had two gender roles in the '50s, butch and *femme*. I wasn't butch so therefore I had to be *femme*. If I were young now, in the world that abounds with a wider variety of role models, would I emulate a more androgynous star like k. d. lang?

Learning that my awkward childhood is a universal gay experience helped me feel better about myself. It's reassuring to know I wasn't the first kid in the world to act 'girly' and won't be the last. Todd Haynes' fabulous movie, *Dottie Gets*

Spanked, the story of a young gay boy living in New York in the '50s, taught me that many gay boys around the world endured similar childhoods. Despite our radically different home towns — you can't get much further from Puhoi than New York — Haynes' hero endures the same hostility I experienced. He wants to sit by the girls in the school bus and talk movie stars, fashions and dolls, but they reject him. He spends all his time drawing beautiful women with long eyelashes and *bouffant* hair-dos. His Mom is confused. His Dad looks angry — as mine did one night when he came into the bathroom and found me playing movie stars in a bubble bath. He said, 'You little queen.'

In 1962, when I was aged 10, we moved to the Golconda Hotel in Coromandel. Coromandel, with a dozen shops, seemed like a huge town to us. Dad prospered. As Nana said, 'He achieved all his aims in life. He owned hotels and race horses.'

Nana was a marvellous matriarch who controlled a tight-knit family web comprising her eight children, their partners and 36 grandchildren. She was a wonderful grandmother, but must have been a challenge as a mother-in-law. She was the one person who never made me feel bad about my 'girly' pursuits and who never expected me to play rugby — in fact she actively encouraged me not to play that rough, horrid game. She also fostered my love of the movies, theatre and music. She and I would sit up in her bed and speak and sing our way through the entire book of *My Fair Lady*.

The kids at my new school, and then my siblings, started to call me 'girly'. It was the worst name you could be called, and I know why they did it. I cried easily. I had a high voice. I hated rough games. I was obviously not the most butch of children.

None of the adults around me ever discussed the name-calling. The closest Mum came to mentioning it was when I hit my brother, after he'd been teasing me. When he complained to Mum, she said, 'Well, you shouldn't call him "girl" all the time.' But she never said anything directly to me about it. Although I was bullied, and suffered from migraines, shingles and hives, I don't remember my childhood as being unhappy.

When I was 12 I was sent away from home, to be a third form boarder at Sacred Heart College, Glen Innes, a Marist Brothers school. I didn't like it very much. None of the other boys at school enjoyed being there either, but we didn't run away or rebel. Kids were more docile in those days.

Although I was in the top stream all through high school I never felt particularly clever. I was usually in the bottom half of the class. I had a best friend, Joseph (not his real name because he's still very closeted). Strictly speaking, we shouldn't have been friends — he was a year ahead of me — but we gravitated to one another. We both loved films, the Kinks, Dusty Springfield and *Playdate* magazine. We didn't realise it then, but we were both gay.

My other two best friends were Ted and Graeme, my cousins, whom I saw during the school holidays. They were all the things I wasn't: popular, brave, butch and sensible. They had girlfriends and cars. Nana said, 'Graeme got all the charm. Ted got all the commonsense. I don't know what you got, Jimmy.'

I felt everyone was better than me, so took revenge by sneering at everyone and everything. My sarcasm and nastiness were a sign of my complete unhappiness. I remember visiting my Uncle Peter and Auntie Bernice's brand new home. It was just the sort of house I'd have loved to live in — on a cliff-top overlooking a wonderful beach, with big ranchslider doors, leather chairs and a stunning kitchen. Instead of admiring it, I strutted about saying how awful it was. How my uncle and aunt held back from clocking me one, I'll never know. My life is crowded with embarrassing memories of unpleasant incidents like this, where I savaged people whose only crime was to make me feel second-rate and jealous.

But I'm digressing ... At school the highlight of the week came on Saturday afternoons, when it was mandatory to watch the First Fifteen play rugby. I always hated rugby. I was the only boarder who refused to play. As a punishment the Master of Discipline gave me the job of marking out the rugby fields with those white sticks at the 25 yard, 50 yard, 75 yard and goal lines. Sacred Heart had about 16 football fields, so I spent many winter days lugging sticks around muddy, icy fields.

My favourite part of school was the dramatic society. This was a legitimate chance to be dramatic, to posture and pout, wear make-up and have fun. Brother Chanel was a keen and encouraging director, and we did everything from Gilbert and Sullivan operettas to Shakespeare.

Growing up I'd enjoyed the usual sexual explorations that kids indulge in. It's as natural a part of growing up as learning to walk and talk, but these days, if Social Welfare finds out about it, kids get sent off to counsellors. This childish sex play stopped around the age of 10 or so.

Sexually speaking, Sacred Heart was in total denial. Sex was banned. Our personal reading had to be approved by the Brothers. There was no TV. We did have movies in the gym on Saturday nights, but if there was kissing a Brother would put his hand over the projector lens so we couldn't see. I knew nothing about masturbation, gay or straight sex. I never talked about sex with Joseph. The fact he might be gay never entered my head. We never had a physical relationship. The first sexual inkling I had was seeing a photo, in *Life* magazine, of a handsome Australian lifesaver walking along the beach. For some reason, I didn't really consider why, the tanned hunk in the tiny Speedos fascinated me. Thirty years later I can recall his photograph perfectly.

One day, in fourth form, the chaplain took me out of class and over to the chapel where, in a very awkward way, he told me Dad was dead, starting with 'Your father's had an accident' and building up to a muttered 'Yes', when I asked, 'Is he dead?' At no stage did he physically comfort me, even though I was crying my eyes out. How could anyone, I now wonder, tell a boy his father's dead and not comfort him with a hug and a cuddle?

The last time I saw Dad was in the bar of the Station Hotel, a cigarette and a beer in either hand, surrounded by boozy mates. He stuck a £20 note in my blazer pocket and waved me off to school. With his hefty size — he was around 16 stone, I guess — and his diabetic condition, it's no wonder he had an early heart attack. He had a huge funeral, with several hundred mourners.

Mum was devastated. She had seven children still at home, aged from 13 down to one Nana took the two smallest to live with her and Mum bravely ploughed on, running the hotel, holding the family together.

Back at school I, along with most of the fourth formers, hit puberty — or did it hit us? Masturbation became *the* big topic. Of course I tried it, though at first I couldn't ejaculate. Sex was a mystery for Catholic kids. We never had any sex education but priests were always lecturing us about the mortal sin of touching yourself. Do it, and you went to hell. 'By spilling your seed,' one priest told me in Confession, 'you're a murderer, killing all those potential lives that could be coming into the world. You don't want to be a murderer, do you?'

During the warm spring weeks that closed that school year, another fourth former seduced me. Tom — I won't use his real name because I have no idea where he is or what he does, and have no desire to 'out' someone 30 years on — was handsome, a tough, stocky footballer from a lower-streamed manual class. Young, dumb and full of cum, as they say. I know people tend to idealise their first lovers, but his photo in the school magazines proves he really was hot stuff, even by today's rigorous standards of male beauty.

I can't recall what signal he gave me, or even what made us aware of one another, but one Saturday night we slipped away from the gym. Tom took me up to our dormitory, which was really risky. There was no privacy. If a Brother had come in we'd have been spotted instantly. We got into his bed and played with each other. He was incredibly well-endowed and he had lots of pubic hair. I was totally impressed. At this stage all I had was a practically pre-pubescent acorn. For the next three years we met all over the school: under the gym (I'd been given a key to this locked area — the rugby sticks were kept here — so my punishment had its silver lining), in the toilets, the dormitories, behind buildings. We had sex — mutual masturbation only — here, there and everywhere.

We didn't talk much when alone together and totally ignored each other in public. I never mentioned our liaisons to anyone. I never even thought about them, really. I didn't identify them as gay sex, or even as sex. It was a part of my life in a little cupboard all on its own, not related to any other part of my life. Tom left at the end of the lower sixth form. I stayed on for seventh form. I didn't miss him. Didn't yearn for him. Didn't look for other sex partners. The sex happened because he was there, and when he left I didn't think about it at all.

During my last year at school I became close friends with two other boys. All three of us were gay, but we weren't out and never discussed sex. We'd sneak out of school and drive around Glen Innes shopping centre in a Fiat Bambina, taking turns pretending to be Miss New Zealand, standing up and waving through the sunroof at the suburban shoppers. Fifteen years later, when we came out to one another, I learned they'd also been having sex with other boys. But we'd all compartmentalised our lives, putting our sexual exploits into a very secret corner, a fairly standard response to society's hostility towards gay sex.

I left high school with an A Bursary and the maturity level with which I'd entered — that of a 12-year-old. Sacred Heart did nothing to encourage maturity. We followed orders, or else we got caned. I started Law School at Auckland, totally ill equipped for life in the real world.

For the next 14 years my life could be a movie called 'The Years Of Living Aimlessly', in which I drop out, drug up, freak out and sober up. During these years I lived in about 200 dreary flats in Auckland, Sydney, London and Los Angeles. I drifted through numerous occupations: university student, ATI student, student teacher, warehouseman, factory worker, bookshop assistant, porn shop assistant, kitchen hand, waiter, movie extra, tractor driver, bus driver, fruit picker, delivery man, computer operator, telephonist, receptionist, house boy, cleaner, gym assistant and dole-bludger.

At university I met up with Joseph, who was very involved with the anti-war culture and the drug culture. Desperate to be part of the gang, I followed along. I marched against the war and slept on the floor of a dirty Grafton Road commune house. I smoked marijuana, took LSD and anything else I could get my hands on.

When we first started taking LSD the 'trips' were treated as semi-religious experiences, a buzzy high for intellectual university students. Everyone read Carlos Castenada, all about seeing the face of God, and we would put together little 'tripping' kits, with gauzy scarves, flowers and kaleidoscopes. This pretentiousness didn't last. Before long LSD became just another party drug, and soon we were dropping acid to go see Mama Cass play Witchie Poo in *Puff'n'Stuff* at kiddie matinees.

Around this time I nearly killed myself with anti-depressants. Looking for a cheap pharmaceutical high, I followed the druggie trail to a well-known doctor with rooms in Parnell. I got a prescription for a popular brand of anti-depressants and stupidly took the whole lot, expecting to get really stoned. Instead I collapsed in St Stephen's Avenue and my heart stopped, several times. I was rushed by ambulance to Auckland Hospital, resuscitated, had my stomach pumped and was interviewed by the police. Groggily I explained I'd overdosed just for fun. I was released the next morning. I was so stupid that I boasted about the whole affair, not appreciating just how foolish I had been.

If overdosing was something of a rite of passage in the early '70s, it was the only rite of passage I successfully negotiated. Compared to everyone else I knew, I felt a real failure. Joseph, Ted and Graeme all had good careers, lots of friends, and serious girlfriends. I still hadn't got a life or a lover. I was a tubby, immature, over-excitable adolescent with no girlfriend and no exam passes for my first year. I lost my bursary and found work in a bookshop warehouse.

I refused to face the fact I might be gay. I had several awkward sexual encounters with guys met quite by chance, and kept hoping that a beautiful woman would come into my life and make me heterosexual. Guess what? She did! My friend Jean got a new flatmate, a training college student called Veronica — not her real name, but wherever she is and whatever she's doing, I'm sure she doesn't want to be dragged into my little *histoire d'amour*. Veronica was beautiful and impulsive, with a blonde crew cut and an outrageous dress sense, the Courtney Love of her era. She'd just broken up with her boyfriend, and on the rebound she and I somehow fell into bed together and she seduced me.

I was on the top of the world. I don't think there's anyone happier than a gay man, frightened of being gay, who manages a successful heterosexual sexual performance. A couple of weeks later, at a cousin's wedding, we announced our engagement. I thought our love would last for ever. It turned out to have a six-month expiry date.

Veronica encouraged me to apply for training college. She also encouraged me to audition for an amateur production of a gay play, *The Boys in the Band*. I got the part of Cowboy and, for the first time, became involved with a group of out gay men. Almost immediately I started an affair with another actor, Peter. One day Veronica came home and found us in bed together. Peter and I leapt out of bed, pulled on our jeans and joined Veronica who was sitting, stunned, at the kitchen table. I made the introductions.

'Veronica, darling, this is Peter. Peter, meet my fiancée.' No one said anything. 'Let's have a cup of tea,' I said, and proceeded to boil, brew and pour while Veronica and Peter stared at each other. I moved out shortly after.

In 1975, after four years of warehouse and shop work, I started training college, and for the first time since high school my life felt focused. Training college was the best thing that ever happened to me — the successful high school experience I didn't have at Sacred Heart. Although most of the students were 17 and I was 23, we were at the same level of maturity and I fitted right in. In PE classes we were taught how to do those simple things I'd never learnt, like how to throw a ball. I felt physically confident for the first time in my life — so much so I joined a gym and have worked out regularly ever since.

This physical and social confidence gave me, finally, the emotional confidence to make a decision about my sexual orientation. Although I now had gay friends, I was still so anxious about being gay I couldn't discuss my coming out with them. It was something I had to do independently. I see coming out as an adventure you take on your own, then you come back and tell everyone about your journey. So I went and saw the training college counsellor, Father Felix Donnelly's sister, and she sent me along to see Felix. He gently introduced the idea that I might be gay and that perhaps the heterosexual ideal of a wife and a family were not for me.

After a few months counselling I was ready to tell someone I was gay. At this time I was sharing a house with my cousin Ted and his wife Jules, a wonderfully warm, loving woman. One afternoon I spent a long time slowly coming out to her and she was really supportive. Coming out is so difficult the first few times you do it. They're crucial moments.

I next came out to John Pound and Gib Rogers, two cast members from *The Boys in the Band*. They had their own house in Glen Innes, and I practically moved in with them. John and I were soul mates. We knew each other inside out, confided everything and supported one another. Through Father Donnelly I became involved in a gay men's discussion group where I met my other 'best' friend, Richard Davies. A successful high school rower, Richard was tall, muscular, handsome. We went flatting together. We were close — he'd sit in the bath and I'd shave his shoulders — but never sexually attracted to each other. Richard and John and I laughed, partied and cruised together.

I had a few flings, but didn't have the overwhelming emotional and physical experience of making love with a man I loved madly until I met Keith. (Once again, I'm not using his name because his mother doesn't want me to write about him. This is the last time I'm not using someone's real name. See what happens when you live in a closet? You drag everyone else in with you.)

Keith and I met at one of the coffee evenings run by my gay men's group, a safe place for gay men to meet outside the pubs, saunas and public toilets. He was handsome, worldly, wealthy and a marvellous chef. When we first made love I fainted from passion. This was love and I was ecstatic.

Keith wasn't perfect, though. Despite his smooth exterior, he and I were very similar — insecure, defensive, still coming out as gay men — and two insecure, sarcastic people make great sparring partners but not great lovers. Although we started out with excellent rapport and sexual chemistry, we destroyed it all through having dreadful arguments.

Meeting Keith gave me the impetus to come out to my mother. I visited her during the August holidays of my first year teaching. I got up early one morning and had a cup of tea with her in the kitchen before anyone else was up. I told her that I'd fallen in love with Keith and we were going to England together. She took the news calmly and supportively, as she always does.

In England I got a job in the Grosvenor House Hotel health club, a glamorous gym where stars like Liza Minnelli, Farrah Fawcett, Christopher Reeve and Bianca Jagger work out. I'd always been fascinated by stars, and it was disappointing to see them up close.

Keith and I were quickly falling apart as a couple. We quarrelled a lot and we were both secretly having casual sex outside the relationship. Casual sex in London meant cruising the parks and public toilets. I wasn't at all keen on public toilets, but the parks were a different matter. Hampstead Heath at night is a magical place — a forested hillside filled with hundreds of men. Trolling the trails of the Heath, I'd chance upon all sorts of gay men doing their thing: a gang of leather boys tying each other to trees, very *avant garde*; some suburban dad-types kissing like teenagers; a posse of cowboys encircling a gorgeous naked stud.

In London's Green Park I had one of the most marvellous sexual encounters of my life, with a young Italian kitchen-hand. At least I guess he was a kitchen-hand, perhaps from the Ritz Hotel over the fence, because he was in kitchen whites. Our eyes met, our bodies followed and, although we couldn't speak a word of each other's language — in fact, I don't think we even attempted to speak — we intuitively pleasured each other. No wonder gays become addicted to casual sex. You can have some marvellous adventures. Of course, you can also have some awful, degrading ones. For a couple of years I found it thrilling and liberating. Needless to say, I was just following the crowd.

While frustrated heterosexuals were reading about zipless fucks in Erica Jong's *Fear of Flying*, gay men were living out that particular dream on the streets of San Francisco and the wharves of New York, in the Tuileries Gardens of Paris and on the crumbling edges of the Circus Maximus in the centre of Rome — where, on drowsy, dusty Sunday afternoons, hidden beneath clumps of oleander bushes, with hordes of camcorder-toting tourists only a few metres away, handsome, olive-skinned Roman gladiators indulge in unarmed combat. Of course, every generation thinks it invented sex. Gore Vidal says he and his boyfriends invented it in the '40s.

Part of this sexual hysteria was the constant parade of sexual disease that went with it: crabs, syphilis, gonorrhoea, genital and anal warts, herpes, hepatitis, throat infections, amoeba infections, to name just a few that I suffered from at one time or other. All the gay men I knew were constantly at the venereal diseases clinic giving blood samples, being swabbed, disinfected and penicillined. None of us took much notice of this constant toll on our immune systems. We were all young, gorgeous and going to live for ever. Besides, we went to the gym. Surely that was being health-conscious enough.

When my Aunt Doris died and left me a couple of thousand dollars I fled England for Sydney, Australia. Although Keith and I were living in different time zones, we didn't officially break up. Ostensibly I was filling in time until we set up house again in New Zealand.

Sydney, like training college, was a quantum leap forward

in my personal development. It had a terrific gay community. I moved into a sunny Surry Hills terrace house with three other gay guys, Mike, Lindsay and Brian, who became an instant family. We did everything together. I hung out with Richard, my old Newmarket flatmate, who now lived in Sydney. At last, I felt I belonged!

Of course, I fucked it all up. I was working in The Love Shop, a sex shop in Kings Cross, and one night the police came in and arrested me for selling pictures of people having sex with animals. I'd never noticed the books in the store before. I appeared before the magistrate charged with selling pornography. I was found guilty, but the conviction was not recorded because I had no prior record. Frightened by the entire experience, I flew back to New Zealand that afternoon. I moved back in with Keith, in his smart Ponsonby cottage, and went on the dole. I occasionally cleaned houses or waited tables, but spent most days at the gym and in front of TV.

Keith and I slept in separate rooms. We were going nowhere fast and I decided that it was time we broke up for good. My plan was to move back to Sydney. My two ambitions: (1) to sleep with as many cute guys as possible; (2) to become a receptionist at a smart hotel.

I left Keith's and moved in with an old school friend, Daniel. After a few years on the move, all my worldly goods fitted into one suitcase. I paid my way by cleaning, ironing and cooking for Daniel. I was 30 and my life was truly down the tubes. I had no career. I was too old to train for anything. I had applied for the journalism course at ATI, because I'd always fancied being a writer, but was turned down as too old.

An Auckland city magazine called *Metro* had recently been launched. It was witty and amusing and I tried writing a humorous piece for it, comparing the people of Ponsonby, Mt Roskill and Remuera. The editor, Warwick Roger, liked it. I heard nothing more. I kept up the house cleaning, going to the gym and saving my dole money to pay my fare to Sydney.

In June 1983, just turned 31, at the point in my life when I'd decided there was no such thing as true love, I met Kim, and fell in love more deeply than I ever dreamed possible. This is how it happened. John and I went to Alfie's, *the* gay night club, one Friday night, and I saw this very cute guy arrive with two friends of mine, Peter and David. I rushed over and said, 'Who's that?' Turns out he's Peter's cousin, coming out on the Auckland scene for the first time. I tried to make conversation, but Kim had mustered up the courage to come out by drinking far more than usual and he was pretty out of it.

The next Friday night Kim was there again, standing alone on the side of the dance floor. 'Remember me?' I said. He didn't. I asked him to dance and, at the end of the first song — probably *Wake me up before you Go-Go* by Wham!, which played relentlessly in 1983 — he didn't walk off, which is what usually happened. Instead, we kept dancing. John gave me the V for Victory sign across the dance floor.

A week later we had our first date — dinner at a pizza place in Dominion Road. Kim picked me up in his car but I felt, as the older guy, that I should pay for everything. Which was tough, because I only had about $17 — I was still on the dole. I bought a cheap bottle of white wine, gave Kim a glass at home, then took the bottle to the restaurant. I could only afford one pizza to share.

Over the next few months Kim and I went through the dating and courting process. I was so emotionally wound up in our affair that, for the first time, I had difficulty with the physical act of love-making. I was so tense I couldn't perform. It was like being a virgin all over again.

Kim's love and respect gave my self-esteem a gigantic boost. He also ended my years of aimless drifting. He was the first person to sit down with me and say, 'What do you want to be? Work out what it is and start working towards that goal. Define your goal.' I had never had a goal before. I decided I was keen to try for a career as a writer. I wrote another story 'on spec' for *Metro*, about the gay community from the point of view of a gay man. Warwick bought it and commissioned another.

Within a couple of months my life had turned around. Suddenly I had a lover and a career path. Now, when Kim introduced me to his family, I could say I was a freelance journalist, rather than an unemployed teacher.

Kim's family life was a total revelation. The respect he brought to our relationship was a reflection of the respect his family had for each other. Kim and his three brothers, all very close in age and outlook, were good friends and spent a lot of their time together. I hadn't lived at home for nearly 20 years and had lost touch with my brothers and sisters. We were widespread in age and outlook. When we met, we didn't communicate effectively.

Our first Christmas together, Kim and I had a holiday in India. I paid my way with the insurance money from a burglary at Keith's house just before I moved out. During our trip Kim and I really got to know and depend on each other. By the time our Indian summer was over, I couldn't leave him and return to Sydney.

Back in Auckland, though, I had nowhere to live — Daniel had emigrated to England. Kim's parents invited me to move

in with them. Their generosity amazes me to this day —
though it's very much a reflection of the love and support
they have for their children.

As I got to know Kim's social circle, my behaviour was
not, initially, all it should have been. Becoming Kim's partner
catapulted me a couple of dozen rungs up the social ladder,
and I was insecure and awkward in my new position. I found
some of his friends and relations overpowering at first, and
behaved badly, falling back on my old ways of insult and
sarcasm as a defence against anyone who made me feel
second best. Over the years, thanks to Kim's encouragement,
I've grown in confidence. Still, it's taken a long time to let
go of the anger and the insecurity of my early years.

After a year with his parents, Kim and I moved into our
own home and began the exhausting process of renovating
and rebuilding. After 12 years we now have a beautiful house
that's very much a reflection of Kim's love of order, balance
and harmony.

We have an excellent relationship. He's done so much for
me, but sometimes I wonder what I've done for him. On
bad days I think, 'I've done nothing to deserve this
happiness. I'm just an interloping carpetbagger.' On good
days I look around our house and feel some credit for our
clean, well-run home. My domestic career has priority over
my writing career, which soared beyond all my expectations.
After a five-year apprenticeship at *Metro*, Warwick hired me
full-time. Two years later I moved to *Fashion Quarterly*, as
the features editor. *FQ* was a very unhappy office. Most days
someone was in tears. After two years I quit and went
freelancing — financially insecure work I can pursue thanks
to Kim's financial support. I work at home all day and make
sure Kim comes home every night to a tidy house with

dinner cooked, the bed made, the clothes washed and ironed.

When we first got together I encouraged Kim to be as sexually adventurous as I had been. The gay ethos at the time held that gay couples shouldn't be monogamous. It was seen as a pathetic attempt to ape a heterosexual lifestyle. I didn't want to repress Kim and have him say in 20 years, 'I missed out!' But he preferred a monogamous relationship. That's how it's been from the very beginning, and we've always been very comfortable with it. Falling in love, and into a steady relationship, in 1983 is the reason I'm still here in 1995, when all my old flatmates are dead and gone.

In May 1984 my best friend ever, John Pound, called. He was very upset. I rushed over to his house. He hugged me very close and said, 'The doctor thinks these purple lumps in my throat are AIDS.' I pretended to push him away and said, 'Couldn't you have told me by telegram?' We made everything into a joke. Then we both cried.

AIDS. We'd only heard about this disease a year or so earlier, and now John had it. He wasn't too ill at first, but after a year or so he got purple Kaposi's sarcoma lesions all over his face and body. KS lesions were untreatable at this time, and he started to rot where the lesions were at their worst — on his nose and his toes. He decayed rapidly. Parts of his body swelled and bloated, his skin flaked off. He lost a frightful amount of weight. He could barely walk. You'd hold him up and he'd take these tiny, halting steps. It could take 10 minutes to cross the living room. His eyesight went. He was lucky — his family rallied round and nursed him.

I had another shock when Richard, my other best friend, showed me the big purple lesions all over his arms. Like John, Richard died at home, cared for by friends, but unlike John, who was sane to the end, Richard developed encephalitis (water on the brain), toxoplasmosis (brain abscesses) and dementia. Mid-1986 my two best friends died within two months of each other.

No sooner had I got over their deaths than Steve, my best English friend, wrote to tell me that both he and his lover Ross were ill with AIDS. Ross died first, then Steve. I talked to Steve by phone during his last days. He was totally blind.

A year or so after Steve's death I heard from the last three members of my small gay family, my old Aussie flatmates Michael, Lindsay and Brian. They too were sick from HIV-related illnesses. I immediately flew to visit them. With AIDS, you learn to respond quickly. A day's delay can be too late.

Michael died first, courageous to the end in the face of a cruel series of illnesses that left him emaciated and blind. Lindsay, Michael's partner of 12 years, cared for Michael during his last days. Lindsay then faced, with incredible bravery, the prospect of his last few days alone. He died six months later, blind and delirious.

Brian just vanished. Letters came back marked, 'Gone. No forwarding address.' I can only assume he's dead.

Time is supposed to heal everything but, a decade later, I feel more upset about these deaths than I did when they occurred. I realise I'll never make such close friendships again. The friendships we make as young adults, sharing adventures as we explore the world and our place in it, are unique. When you're older, in a steady relationship, settled in your own home, there are too many barriers to creating new, intimate friendships. All my old, best friends are dead. Every day I realise what I'm missing by not having them around, and feel their loss more keenly.

Paul Sherriff

I was born on 14 August 1961, in Temuka, South Canterbury. Mum was 19, and Dad, a dairy farmer's son working on the family farm, was 20. The maternity hospital's gone now, replaced by an old people's home, where my grandfather lives. His grandfather was one of three brothers, all convicts, transported from England to Tasmania.

I'm the oldest of four kids, two boys and two girls, all close in age. We're fourth-generation New Zealanders and our family has always lived in the Clandeboye/Milford district, near Temuka. It's a very conservative district — I'm one of its most liberal products by far.

Clandeboye/Milford was strongly Presbyterian. Although Dad's Presbyterian, Mum's Catholic — which meant we were brought up Catholic and signed up for a lifetime of guilt. Catholics were considered second rate back then, though I never noticed any prejudice. But I've heard since about people who thought the Sherriffs were lovely kids but who couldn't get over us being Catholic.

I grew up in an extended family situation, influenced as much by my grandparents as my parents. Grandad still worked on the farm, and he and Nanna lived just down the road. Families of cousins farmed nearby as well. As the favourite child I could do no wrong — which pleased me, but not my siblings and cousins. In those days the responsibility of maintaining a family's good name went to the senior woman in a family, which meant Nanna ruled our roost. Mum's never said a word, but my aunties tell horror stories about Nanna the dictator! She never mentioned our convict ancestry, and flew into a rage when my sister asked about it once.

I have wonderful memories of my childhood: playing by the river that ran through our farm; crisp, frosty, winter mornings; running round the grassy paddocks; helping with the cows: all very wholesome and Enid Blyton. I was closer to Mum than to Dad. He and I are quite different, and he was closer to my sister.

My hobbies were electronics and photography. I was inventive and loved pulling things apart then rebuilding them. I worked out how to bug our telephone, which was on a party line, and could monitor calls at home and at the neighbours'. At Guy Fawkes I'd wire sky-rockets up to an electric ignition system, so I could press a button and a sky-rocket would fire off. I learnt morse code, semaphore, and Mum thought I'd be a technician or a scientist.

I went to Dad and Nanna's old school, Milford Primary, a three-room school just down the road. Nanna encouraged me to do well at school, and I made sure that she saw me doing well. The same with my parents. I've always presented the right image to the right people. I suppose I was putting up facades from quite an early age, really.

I then went to Temuka District High School. I enjoyed science and geography classes, became a lab monitor, a librarian, and joined the photography club so I could avoid the teachers on patrol at interval and lunchtime. The last thing I wanted was someone telling me to pull my socks up. Who did they think they were? I wasn't a true rebel in that I certainly wanted to be successful at school, but I questioned the teachers' rights of absolute control. My mother encouraged us to be autonomous and make our own decisions from a very early age.

The authoritarian teachers didn't like me because I wasn't interested in obediently doing things their way. Throughout my life I've encountered people in authority who have disliked me because they suspected I was rigging the system and therefore smugly humouring them.

I passed School Certificate no trouble. University Entrance was a bit more traumatic. Either you were accredited or you had to sit. Throughout the year the teachers kept saying, 'If you don't do this assignment we won't accredit you.' I'd reply, 'Don't accredit me then,' which infuriated them. Accrediting was their big stick and I was taking it out of their hand.

Accrediting passes were announced at an end-of-year meeting attended by all the sixth form students. The teachers went through the class rolls, calling out the names of those who'd passed. It was a scene of public humiliation, with people crying and breaking down. When they didn't call my name, I laughed heartily. However, by sitting and passing UE, I ultimately made a complete farce of the evaluation process, discrediting the teachers and their system.

I tended to socialise with older kids and, in sixth form, started going to the pub with them, despite being terrified the police might raid the place. A teacher spotted me and said, 'I never want to see you here again.' I replied, 'Well, don't come here again.' I usually kept my school authority battles from my parents, but this time I told Mum a teacher had banned me from the pub. She hit the roof. How dare anybody tell her son what to do? 'Who do they think they are?'

My reputation at school was so low that the teachers scoffed at my application to be an American Field Service exchange student, and were furious when I won a scholarship to go the States for my seventh form year. They even held an emergency staff meeting to oppose my selection.

I spent 1979-1980 in Detroit, Michigan, with a wonderful family. I got on very well with my American Dad, an electrical contractor. We were both practical men. I didn't get on quite so well with my American Mom. I think she smelt a bit of a rat, and decided this boy's not quite as angelic as he comes across.

I hadn't considered life after high school. I didn't know what I wanted to do with my life. University never crossed my mind, but everyone in Detroit was going on to university so, back home, I decided to try that. Filling in time until the year began, I worked as a welder at the Timaru coolstores before switching to a great job at Wattie's — 12 weeks driving a pea-vining machine, out in the sunshine all day. I love the sun. At summer's end I shocked the family by announcing, 'I'm not going to university. I'm going to Europe instead.' They preferred university, but my mind was made up. I was 18 and determined not to spend my life saying, 'I wish I'd done that when I was young.'

First I flew to Sweden to see Ulva, a Swedish girlfriend I'd met in Detroit. I moved in with her family and worked as a gardener at her father's factory. Ulva's family were a big shock. The Swedes are very open. There's no bathroom/toilet barrier. Everyone just strolls in and out of the bathroom. First thing in the morning, Ulva's mother would walk past the door completely nude and jump into the shower. Ulva might be sitting on the bidet; her father lying in the bath; her brother brushing his teeth; her little sister on the loo — and they're all chatting. Me, I had to have the bathroom to myself before I could do any one of those things! After a while, though, I learnt to jump into the shower and not care if someone else was in the bathroom. I've been completely cured of any ablution anxiety.

Ulva and I Eurailed around Europe for a couple of months. In 1982 I came home and started an agricultural science degree at Massey, rather than at Lincoln College, only 100 kilometres from our place. Since I anticipated spending a lifetime farming in Temuka, I thought it'd be nice to visit the North Island. I'd toured Europe, but I'd only seen Wellington twice and changed planes at Auckland once.

At Massey, most of the kids were straight from seventh form, whereas I'd seen the world. It wasn't easy socialising with kids whose main desire was to drink themselves stupid. Everyone was into sports, too, something that hadn't previously interested me. I'd always been much happier messing about down the back of the farm, blowing things up or shooting things. I liked watching the All Blacks on TV but never thought about playing myself — probably because Nanna never told me to become an All Black. Feeling left out, I took up cycling and squash and, by the time I finished my degree, I enjoyed several social sports. I played rugby, squash and went jogging. I started aerobics classes and became an instructor. My current interest is weight training.

But I'm getting ahead of myself. In 1984 I completed a Bachelor of Agricultural Science, which covers a wide range advanced skills — economics, management, engineering and sciences — and opens up a number of career options.

That summer Ulva came over from Sweden, but she was a changed woman from the warm, friendly person I'd known. I'm not sure why. There had been several traumatic events in her family, including the death of her brother, so she may have still been working through those. I'd told everyone how wonderful she was, but she was nothing like they expected. My mother had been expecting to welcome her new daughter-in-law, and here was a very angry, ungrateful, surly woman. When she went to dinner at my friends' houses she'd stop eating halfway through the meal and say, 'I don't like this. Can you cook something else?'

We took off for a planned four-month holiday, cruising around Australia, but it was very difficult travelling with someone who disagreed with everything I said and who wanted to do the opposite of everything I wanted to do. Within a week we'd had a big row and I never saw her again. When we separated I was relieved for two reasons: one, that this unpleasant person was no longer around, and two, on a deeper emotional level, I was off the hook so far as doing the right thing and getting married was concerned. Everyone assumed I'd been left at the altar and felt sorry for me. I felt as if I'd had a lucky escape. I'm sure my inner conflict over my sexual orientation made me hold back from fully committing to our relationship. No matter how much I wanted to fall in love with a woman, there was always something inside that stopped me. Maybe Ulva picked up on this unresolved conflict and was angry I was leading her on. I don't know, because we never discussed it. I tried not even to think about it.

Back home, I started my farming career, but after a few weeks I knew it wasn't going to work. You're not autonomous on a family farm. I realised my 'modern university ways' would clash badly with my father's traditional farming methods. When the bank declined to lend the money for our planned expansion, my fate was sealed. No one was on my wavelength in Temuka. When I saw an advertisement for a job at the National Party Research Unit based in Parliament, I applied.

At this time the National Party was still suffering from post-Muldoonism and was low in the polls. I was keen on the party, though: I'd been a member since the age of 17. So in June 1986 I moved to Wellington and started work. Jim Bolger had taken over as National's leader a couple of months earlier.

In 1990, several people within the party encouraged me to stand for Parliament. I first sought nomination in the Waitaki electorate, near home, and was surprised, since I thought I'd run a great campaign, not to be successful in getting selected by the National Party. Perhaps I looked too confident and my clothes were too flash. I was defeated by the same small-town, conservative, 'don't-buck-the-system' attitude I'd endured at school. The only other place I knew well was Massey, so I put my name in for Palmerston North. There was some possibility of winning the seat there, because the sitting MP, Labour's Trevor De Cleene, was retiring. This time around I won selection and opened what is probably the worst chapter of my life.

I discovered the National Party structure in Palmerston North to be extremely fragmented, with old grudges, factions and in-fighting. Should one group support me, then others would oppose me. I ended up pulling in a lot of friends from Wellington to help me campaign. Carloads would come up and give a hand. It's wonderful to have such generous, supportive friends, and I'm eternally grateful to them. But these independent efforts put me offside with the party hierarchy, and resignations were threatened. With six weeks still to run, my spirit was broken. I was badly stressed, losing weight, the whole bit. I felt the campaign had gone completely off the rails. It was my lowest point. Despite sterling support from some very good Palmerston North people and outstanding last-minute help from the Manawatu electorate, our side was so fragmented we weren't able to pull it off.

Back in Wellington I took up the post of press secretary to the employment minister but didn't enjoy several aspects of the job so returned to the Research Unit, quite a different place now National was in government. I've worked here ever since, and am happy here. In fact, I'm too happy. I often think, 'Is it nine years since I first started?' Life's too short to sit in the same office for nine years thinking, 'This is great!'

Last year, looking for entrepreneurial alternatives, I started an 0-900 service, Jokeline (0900-45000), and I'm now considering writing a couple of books.

My life seems to have gone in phases — the student phase, the sporting phase, the farming phase, the gym phase, the political candidate phase, the entrepreneurial phase. And I didn't mention the personal development phase, when I did several courses, including a terrific one by John Kehoe, who wrote *Mind Power*. He sparked my interest in mental conditioning, taught me about perception and reality, and refocused my mind.

This was followed by an emotional development phase. Although I've always been very gregarious, people who knew me intimately felt I put up emotional barriers and would say, 'You're cold as a stone.' Of course I did put up barriers — to hide my sexuality.

I've always been very active sexually. I'd had a very sexual childhood. We used to play naughty games with anyone, basically, who'd play naughty games with us. At primary school these were just children's inquisitive games: you had a fiddle with whoever was around. It didn't make much difference if it was a boy or a girl, because neither of you had really developed your sexuality. But I must say that, looking back, some of my fantasies were male-orientated, and I often felt closer to guys.

In my teen years I rejected these fantasies as I strived to be everything my grandmothers, and everybody else, wanted me to be. I willingly adopted their expectations and successfully met them. Needless to say, these expectations didn't include sex with guys. I had virtually no contact with guys during my teenage years.

As a teenager and young adult, being part of the 'in crowd' involved lots of scoring, so I was always out there, scoring. But it was heartless scoring, because my heart wasn't in it. While I was having sex with some woman, my mind was actually off with some guy somewhere. Even though I never admitted it, to myself or anyone else, I'd always known, sort of, that I was interested in guys. But I was determined never to pursue this interest, which had been there from my earliest years. I fought it. Lying in bed at night I'd tell myself that I wasn't allowed to think about that side of me. I wasn't allowed to have fantasies about guys.

I kept this rule until I was at university, aged 21. For the first time I began to let my mind do what it had always wanted to do. I increasingly fantasised about sleeping with guys, and this really got me attuned to that side of my sexuality.

When I got to university, and after I'd had a couple of

fleeting fiddles — those fumbling sexual encounters guys who aren't out tend to have where both of you get drunk, have sex and then the next day either pretend nothing at all happened or say, 'Boy, were we pissed last night! I can't believe we did that!' — I became very concerned about my sexuality. I went to a counsellor to see if he could rid me of this scourge. I explained to him that I was having these feelings about men, and he said, 'Well, do you think you should meet someone from the gay community and see whether you might be gay or not?'

'No, of course I don't want to meet anybody from the gay community!' I said, incensed. 'That's the last thing I want to do. I want to be rid of these feelings. Just cure me! Give me electric shock treatment!' I left his office feeling no different sexually than when I went in.

I'd already had quite a number of girlfriends — Ulva wasn't an isolated affair — but around this time one relationship developed more deeply than all the others. For once — for a while, anyway — I wasn't being challenged by male-orientated fantasies while making love. I thought, 'This must be love', and actually believed I could marry this woman and be quite happy. But I ended the relationship because I didn't want the guilt of hearing her say, should the relationship fail, 'I gave up everything for you, and now look what you've done to me.' I wanted her to keep her dignity. I've never felt I could ask someone to give up their career and their life, just to be my 'kept' person, as it were.

I suppose I knew time was running out for my 'straight days'. I knew that I would inevitably form a gay relationship on the side, as it were, and a female partner would have to deal with my sexuality. I didn't want to be responsible for the hurt and betrayal. But I couldn't explain that. The best thing to do was to end the relationship over something else. I really felt dishonest at times, and certainly not worth a female partner's love and commitment, knowing that I was not there for the right reasons. In my relationship now, I'm always trying to make sure my partner fulfils everything he wants to do, so that there's none of this, 'I gave up . . .' or 'You're the reason I never did this . . .'

When I came to Wellington and joined the gym, I was initially quite oblivious to the many gay men there. Occasionally, in the changing room, guys would get mildly excited — not that they were walking around with raging erections or anything. If I noticed this, I assumed their arousal merely a nervous reaction to their embarrassment at public nudity. I never considered they might be gay and over-heating over someone cute. It wasn't until a couple of gym buddies came on to me, not at the gym but elsewhere, that I realised what was going on. These guys weren't the raging gay stud stereotypes, trying to nail anyone they could get their hands on. It wasn't aggressive, like, 'How about it, hot stuff?' or 'Let's go to my place and . . . ?' These were the tamest pick-ups imaginable — the 'would you like a cup of coffee?' kind. But I still wasn't comfortable with that side of my sexuality. I was scared, and rejected them, not because I wanted to, but because I felt I should.

But then something clicked. I don't know what. I must have moved into a new phase, and within a couple of months I had contact with two or three guys. It was quite innocent stuff. Then, shortly after, I met my partner, Paul.

I met Paul at the gym. We were both training to be aerobics instructors. First time I saw him, I thought, 'Gosh, he's a nice-looking man.' I found myself feeling very attracted to him, but told myself, 'He's not gay. No way is he gay. He's very straight.'

Paul *was* very straight and staunch, and of course, *I* was very straight and staunch too. We started working out together. He'd drop me off after the gym because he lived just up the road, and I'd say, 'Do you want to come up for a cuppa?' But he never would. He now says that he was too scared to because he was feeling the same as me.

One Thursday night, about three months after we first met, we went out drinking and got really drunk. It was very late when we got home, and Paul actually came in. For some reason we started doing aerobics routines in the lounge, very drunk, and woke up all my flatmates, who told us to shut up. So we quietened down. Paul was lying on the sofa, complaining about a sore back, so I said, 'Do you want me to massage your back?' For us, at the time, this was just such a forward thing to say I can't believe I actually said it. He said, 'Yes', took off his shirt and I massaged his back and . . . Anyway, he stood up and I could see he'd really enjoyed his massage. And he could see that I had too. We ended up standing there, looking at each other, thinking, 'Hell! What's going on here? What do we do now?'

Paul said, 'We can't do this in the lounge, we'd better go up to the bedroom.' Without a moment's hesitation we went up to the bedroom and spent the night together — the first night I'd ever spent with a guy.

We were woken in the morning by Matt, my flatmate's boyfriend, coming to see why I hadn't got up for work. Paul and I were too hung-over to get up, and were lying in bed, sort of cuddling, when he walked in. Matt goes, 'He's cuddling your back!' We both pretended to be just waking up, and I said, 'Is he? No, he isn't! Yes he is! Hey, what are you cuddling my back for?' Paul and I hammed it up to convince Matt we'd simply crashed together and Paul must have accidentally rolled over and hugged me. Matt only discovered he'd caught us on our first night together when we came out to him two years later.

We spent the first two years of our relationship totally closeted. I would sneak around to Paul's place at 11 p.m. and climb in his bedroom window. If it was raining, I'd drive up, park the car on a side street, slip on a pair of overalls and sandshoes that I kept in the boot, then walk down to his house. The next morning I'd get up at 6.30, tip-toe out, go home, sneak inside, get back into my own bed, then get up again at 7.30, come downstairs and start the day. Sometimes Paul would stay at my place. My room's upstairs, and to smuggle Paul upstairs we'd walk in tandem so that it sounded like just one person going up. If one of us wanted to go to the toilet, the other had to remain completely still, because we didn't want any noise coming from a supposedly empty bedroom.

We played this game for a long time. In fact, we got so good at deceiving people that we started deceiving each other, secretly playing around with other guys. I should say that at this stage of our relationship we were still, occasionally, having sex with women because it was good for 'the image'. Both of us find certain women attractive and we have no trouble sleeping with them. So occasionally there were 'other women', but then we started cheating with guys as well.

One night I caught him out and he confessed all. In reply I confessed I'd been misbehaving as well. I thought, 'Oh, no! Our relationship's over. It's back to being straight.' It was a very traumatic time, but afterwards our relationship was stronger, much stronger. Amazing, really.

Discussing our situation, we decided we'd been able to cheat each other so easily because we were so closeted. Even though we'd been together for two years, no one knew about our relationship. Our sexuality was a secret between ourselves — and the guys we'd been sleeping with, obviously. But because our casual partners respected our pleas to keep these liaisons in the closet, we knew our secret passions were safe from everyone, especially each other. Paul and I realised that we were more frightened of losing each other through our cheating than we were about everyone learning about our sexuality. We admitted our relationship was the most important thing in our lives and decided the only way to preserve it was to be honest and come out.

Coming out was quite a long process. First of all we came out to our closest friends, to our flatmates and to gay friends we already knew from the gym. Everyone was really wonderful. From the very start my varsity friends have been really accepting of us and our relationship, which is great.

For the first time we were able to go to gay pubs. We also went to Wellington's big Devotion dance party, which was a real buzz. My God, we were wide-eyed and agog at that. The crowd at Auckland's Hero party was even more of an eye-opener, especially the guys in their little Lycra numbers.

Paul and I were now socialising with gay friends at barbecues and parties, and they used to tease us because neither of us knew anything about gay culture. They'd talk about gay icons, like Judy Garland, and we had no idea who they meant. They'd say, 'You're supposed to be gay and you don't know about *The Wizard of Oz*?'

But we still hadn't tackled our families, which we really thought would be a big hurdle.

One night at Caspers, Wellington's main gay club, a barman suggested that Paul and I should enter the Mr Gay Wellington contest. I won. This result was reported in *Man to Man*, New Zealand's national gay newspaper. The mainstream media picked it up, fascinated that 'a National Party researcher', and one-time 'National Party candidate', even entered such a competition, let alone won it. The big focus was my relationship with John Banks, a famously anti-gay National member of Parliament. 'How well do you know John Banks? Is he a friend of yours? Does he know you're gay?'

I said, 'He's now aware that I'm gay, and is comfortable with it.' Actually, I've always got on well with John. When this happened, he didn't know what to say or even how to broach the subject. One day, walking past my office door, he called out, 'Sherriff! I still like you!' Some colleagues were embarrassed for me, but I wasn't embarrassed. This was John's way of dealing with it, and trying to say, 'Yeah, you're okay.' Subsequent to this, we had a conversation and he said, 'Look, for God's sake just be careful. There are some grubby little bastards out there!' I know when he was minister of police he saw some material he found fairly horrific. I assured him I wasn't being manacled in a sling at local leather parties or anything.

Certain gay people give me flak for being friendly to John but I'm not living my life to suit their or anyone else's prejudices. I also get on with Graeme Lee, another anti-gay rights member of Parliament. Graeme comes from a religious angle on all of this, but he's got over the fact I'm gay and is back to his old self.

Back to coming out to my family. I thought they might have guessed about me and Paul, because I'd taken him home for a couple of Christmases and on other occasions. One Easter we went home together and I was hoping for the 'right moment' to come up so I could tell them about being gay and my relationship with Paul, and we'd both be there to talk about it. We had mentally rehearsed coming out to our families so many times. Like in bungy jumping — we were on the edge, ready to jump. But the subject never came up and we left, mildly relieved but annoyed we hadn't raised the subject.

So. It was a Thursday afternoon. I'd just packed my bags and was about to leave for Auckland to take part in the Mr Gay New Zealand competition. Expecting publicity was on its way — possibly enough to reach Temuka — I picked up the phone and I rang home. (My hunch was right. That weekend the *Sunday News* ran a story, with a photograph, on me being gay.)

My sister answered, so I thought, 'I'll practise on her.' I told her I was gay and her response was great. 'Really?' she said. 'That's good. I wish I'd known years ago. We could have all gone out talent spotting together.' Here I am, in major stress mode, ready to go into trauma because I'm about to tell my mother I'm gay, and my sister's making inane comments about how we could have double-dated as teenagers! Finally, Mum came on the phone.

'Mum, I'm about to go up to Auckland,' I said.

'Oh, why?'

'I'm going into the Mr Gay New Zealand competition.'

'Oh, you do some silly things, don't you.'

We chatted on for a bit, then she said, 'Well, where are you staying?'

'They're putting us up somewhere.'

'But you might have to share with a gay man!'

'Well,' I said, 'I fully expect I will.'

And Mum says, 'Oh! Well, perhaps you should pull out.'

I said, 'Oh, it's a bit late for that.'

She didn't really cotton on to what I was trying, in my roundabout way, to tell her, and after some more not-quite-getting-the-point conversation, I rang off.

About 10 minutes later the phone rings. It's Mum.

'Well, I'm not very good at riddles. Are you gay?'

'Yeah.'

She went into minor shock. All she could say was, 'Oh dear, oh dear.'

'I thought you knew,' I said.

She replied, 'Well, mothers don't like to think these things,' which I thought was quite sweet, and probably quite right too. My mother asked about my political future. I told her I'd decided you can't stay in the closet for ever. New Zealand has grown up so much in the last 10 years, being gay is not the big deal it was. To this day, Mum's still not very comfortable with my sexuality, and coming out to her is the only conversation we've ever had about it.

I didn't speak to Dad, leaving it up to Mum or my sister to break the news. Apparently, when he heard, Dad went around saying, 'I can't believe it. I don't know what's happened.' He was more vocal in expressing his reaction.

A few months later Paul and I took our first trip home since dropping this bombshell, to celebrate Mum's birthday. For the first time we'd all be together as a family and 'They know!' We arrived at about 11 at night, and Dad was already in bed. I wondered if he was avoiding us. I hadn't even spoken to him since coming out and had no idea how he'd react to our presence. Mum just chatted away as though there was nothing unusual about having the two of us there.

The next morning we were having breakfast when Dad came in from milking the cows or feeding the pigs or something. He opens the door with a big smile and says, 'Hi! How are you going?' Everything was fine. I thought, 'This is funny.' The whole weekend went really well.

The next time we spoke was on Christmas Day. I called up and spoke to Mum. Fine. I spoke to Dad. Fine. And then he goes, 'Oh, and Merry Christmas to Paul as well.' Mum couldn't say that. She couldn't even mention Paul. But Dad came through, and when he said that, I really felt good. I feel that he's accepted me and Paul, and I'm very pleased.

I think Mum worries, really, about what people will say, which is understandable when you live in a small rural district. They got many phone calls from people who saw me in the news. Surprisingly, some rang up to say, 'Well done!', but others rang up to commiserate. My mother chose to focus on the negative rather than the positive.

Even though I'd told most of my friends about being gay, there was one person who I didn't want to tell — an old and good friend who's very conservative. After the *Sunday News* story, he rang and asked, 'Were you scared to tell me?' I admitted I had been. His reply was, 'Bloody gutsy effort! Well done!'

The whole coming out process has been trouble free. I don't regret it at all. As Chris Carter said when he declared himself in Parliament, 'It's very empowering.' Coming out is such an honest thing to do. You finally feel good about yourself. You're not playing games any more. It's 'Here I am, warts and all. If you've got a problem with that, then please deal with it elsewhere. I'm not your counsellor. I don't need to hear your problems about my sexuality.'

Ravi Sandhu

I was born in Arusha, Tanganyika, in 1953. Tanganyika became Tanzania in 1964, when the island of Zanzibar joined with the mainland under one government. It sounds very romantic, does it not? Spices, cloves, Freddie Mercury . . .

My given name is Ravinderpal, but as I have moved through different stages of life different names have stuck. In India I was called Pappu, a standard Indian name for a boy. When we moved to Uganda in 1962 I became Pal to family and friends, and I am still called this by them. When I started school I became Ravinder, and most of my senior school friends call me this today. In college I became Ravi. Here in New Zealand I became Raavee. [Ravi laughs, pronouncing Ravi with a broad New Zealand accent.] Ravinder would be my favourite name but it is not a practical name for New Zealand. I'm quite happy with Ravi, which is Sanskrit for the sun. I do not know if I am radiant . . .

I was born into an Indian Sikh family, the youngest of four children. Dad was an accountant clerk with the King's African Rifles, and Mum was a housewife. I have two brothers and one sister, all older than me. It's crazy, but we all ended up doing medicine. When I tell people this, they invariably ask if Dad was a doctor too. It was in fact my mother who wanted to be one. However, in those days, it just was not the done thing for a girl to finish high school, let alone go to college. She was married off in 1941 and two years later became a mother. My eldest brother was always her favourite. (They had a love/hate relationship. Even today he finds it very difficult to talk about her objectively.) We others were not made to feel second best, but we knew we were not in the same league. The second son may have resented this, but I do not think I ever did. Neither did my sister, but then she was special, being the only girl in the family. She and I get on very well; we're very close.

Apparently, I was not supposed to have been in this world My mother told me that she was so ill with asthma that the doctor said, 'That's it. No more.' When Mum told me this, I said 'Well, it's not my fault. It was you who did the deed.' She got quite embarrassed.

My father was really thrilled when my sister was born because he had always wanted a daughter. Apparently, when I was born, he was doubly pleased because, as he said, 'Now my daughter will be the only girl.' Little did he know that he was getting half and half!

They're both dead now: Dad died in 1967 and Mum in 1974. I wonder how different my life might have been if they had both been alive.

I do not remember my early childhood much. I was, apparently, a very clingy sort of baby. In 1956 my Mum, my sister and I took off to India. We stayed for six years. This is when I remember having the first knowledge within me that I was gay. I did not have a word for it or anything, but I knew I liked boys.

My first conscious sexual experience was around the age of seven or eight, in a vacant lot next to our house. There were three of us, all little boys, and an older boy of about 13. He could get a hard-on and this was impressive. He wanted me to suck the bloody thing, but I said, 'You suck mine first!' We played a little before Mum called out and we ran home.

We lived in India until I was about nine. There was a lot of sex play at this time, with cousins, the kids next door: anyone was game. I do remember getting an inordinate amount of joy out of it. One time we were playing in the street with a boy from next door, who was about a year older. He asked my sister if I was a boy or a girl. She replied, 'Why don't you go have a look?' He never did.

When I was nine we moved to Uganda. My father started working for a company called D. T. Dobie, the German dealers for Mercedes Benz in East Africa. He was on about £50, which was not much for a family of six. There was never much money, and you knew there was not the money to do special things, but I cannot remember ever feeling left out. We had a really good home life, even though Dad's drinking caused a lot of ruction. It killed him in the end: he died of liver failure. I sometimes wonder what demons he was battling with privately. I was lucky, in that my parents had the accumulated wisdom of three children before me, so life was reasonably good. Mum was the disciplinarian, and she would chastise me severely. I can remember Dad hitting me only once.

There was nothing negative attached to being an Indian in Uganda at this time. The general community was not yet divided along racial lines. None of us felt any different. I had African friends. We played together, went to school together, ate together. It is an existence that, sadly, vanished. The sense of community in Uganda was very special. It is something I have sensed only briefly since. I've found it very occasionally in gay circles. I saw it for a short time in San Francisco, and I came upon it in Hamilton's gay circles. But not in Auckland, until I formed my own gay family.

How can I explain this feeling? You felt safe, any time of the day or night, in your home or on the street. People visited constantly. It was always convenient to do things together. If someone called in at two in the afternoon, it was accepted that they'd stay for afternoon tea. If they called at six, then they would not be allowed to leave without food. We were not rich but Mum had a way of stretching what little we had to accommodate guests. There is a lovely Punjabi word, *barkat*, which encapsulates this sense of the ability to stretch out things. I remember one camping trip when I was about 14. Four of us went to this remote island in Lake Victoria to scout it for a possible school trip later. Here we were welcomed by the local community and treated to the most delicious hospitality one could ever want.

Next week is Diwali, two days before Guy Fawkes. It celebrates Indian New Year and the festival of Laxmi, the goddess of wealth and good fortune. You leave your doors open so that She can visit and shower you with all her wealth. I do not know how much of this is taken seriously, but you never know: if She is in the neighbourhood She may well visit. Part of Diwali involves the giving of gifts to everyone you know. My Dad was president of the local Sikh temple. Hence we knew a lot of people and had a lot of sweets and gifts to give. We received as many in return. About a month before Diwali, women would collect together in someone's courtyard and start making all kinds of sweets and savouries, all the while singing and dancing. Then they would move to another house and start all over again. Thus no one person was left to do everything alone. Near Diwali we would get into the car with Mum, her list and pots of food and gifts. Then we would go visiting and giving away these things. We visited everyone, Hindu, Sikh, Muslim or Christian. They did the same in return: on Id, the Muslim day, and Christmas.

I had no sexual hang-ups then. I do not think I have any now, although for this you may have to ask my lover Rajnish! I am Sikh, and used to wear a turban and everything in those days. Mum and Dad were not strongly orthodox. We were brought up to respect all creeds and follow certain tenets: be good, do good, do unto others, et cetera. I believe in Indian religions it is accepted that you are who you are and you pray to whichever god or goddess you choose. So it was easy growing up from that point of view. In many ways it was an idyllic time. I was never butch, but I did everything that went with being a boy. I would go fishing, tadpoling, climbing trees. I played some sport, although I had to be pushed into it. I was not particularly good at sport but I played tennis and some field hockey. I played with dolls, but I also went mountain climbing, rock climbing and abseiling.

All the neighbourhood boys used to play around with each other, which always felt very normal and natural to me. The boys used to get together and talk of masturbation. This word was not in our argot then, but was easily the most sophisticated one we knew! Yet, deep down, I knew that this was something one did not talk about at home. We had this gang headed by this very tough older boy. He is now a mathematics professor and very much married. Then he was a bit of a lad, and used to play around with the boys. It used to frustrate me, because we never connected sexually. Of our gang, I was easily the youngest and the smallest member. I guess I was protected and cosseted by them. They probably thought I was a bit girly, but I was never treated differently. I could not run as fast or shoot as straight, but I still ran with them, climbed ropes and joined the Boy Scouts.

My family did not shine in sports, unlike another Sandhu family who all ended up representing Uganda at the Munich Olympics in field hockey. But we topped our schools in academics. My eldest brother is brilliant, having topped his class from grade one to final year medical school. He blazed the trail, so everywhere I went I heard, 'Oh, so you are his brother!' Occasionally this was hard to live up to, but it did smooth the path. My second brother was good academically and at sports, but was brilliant at music.

I found primary school very easy. I topped my school in the senior school entrance examinations. High school was a different kettle of fish, although again it was a breeze academically. Suddenly you had to mix with boys and girls from different schools and backgrounds. Like me, most of my friends had older brothers and sisters who had gone before, often studying in the same classes, so a common bond was easily established. At that age, about 12, 13, I was not big or butch. If it came to measuring a degree of masculinity in terms of butch, then I was effeminate. But nobody ever said that, because our entire class would have been classed as effeminate. We were in the top stream every year — the cream. Luckily for us, the standard for excellence in the school was not sport but academic standing. Things have changed. Now you make more money playing basketball than after earning a degree!

In school I was part of the mountaineering club, the Boy Scouts. Every holiday break we would go climbing mountains or camping and hiking. I was often the *chef* for parties of up to 50. From 11 to 18 I would come home on the last day of the term and tell my family, 'Well, I am off.' There were never any hassles. I would pack my rucksack and take off. It was a very free time. We had no chaperones on these trips, which always included boys and girls. We all shared the same tents. Maybe I was oblivious to this, but nothing sexual seemed to go on. Sex, or suspicion of sex, was never a problem, although I am sure things did happen. I was never part of them, unfortunately.

On the other hand, in my first year in high school I started to develop a definite sexual persona. And it was here that I discovered a love for white Jockey underwear. We used to wear shorts to school, and I remember sitting in class one day and looking up the leg of a very attractive friend's shorts and seeing his white Jockeys. They looked delicious. It is a vision I can still conjure up. He looked so beautiful.

Like most gay men, I was very gregarious. You make a unique contribution to the group — not exactly the court jester, but comrade to all, a *bon vivant*. You are everybody's chum, more the girls' than the boys', yet nobody really penetrates the facade you throw up around yourself. I had lots of girlfriends. They were always confiding in me. The boys always looked at me sideways and accepted me, but I knew I did not fit into their scheme of the world. But no one ever said to me, 'You're effeminate.' No one ever said, 'Don't be a girl.' No one ever asked me to not throw like a girl. And I do throw like a girl — underarm! I am really glad I did not go to school in the USA or here.

Just as importantly, I was accepted at home, where it mattered. I remember when I was about nine Dad bought me this rubber pink elephant, the symbol for some tyre company. I loved it, and that elephant went everywhere with me. Mum made some frocks for it. I remember waking up one morning when I was about 15 and thinking, 'My elephant has disappeared.' I was not upset. I must have deliberately put it somewhere and decided it was time to leave it all behind.

Oh God! I remember the first time I came. I was 11 or 12, very naive in these matters, and I thought I was going to burst or my dick was going to fall off and I would become a woman. I did not know which was worse! Fortunately nothing untoward happened and I soon learned to enjoy the pleasures of the hand.

Two major events occurred during my first year in high school. My father died in 1967 and then a few months later I was hospitalised with a paralysing viral illness called Guillain Barré. I was totally paralysed. My lungs worked — nothing else. Mum had to hold my lips shut so I could swallow food. I lay in the hospital bed thinking, 'Shit! This is the last thing my family needs.' With my father's death, we were financially insecure. (Luckily, his life insurance saw us through until my eldest brother qualified as a doctor.) As I lay in bed I remember thinking, 'My family will do anything I ask them to,' but at the same time I concluded, 'I mustn't ask for anything because I don't want to burden them further.' After three months I was lucky enough to make a full recovery — though I had to learn to walk again — and went back to my family, mountaineering and schooling.

This illness marks, for me, the time I really grew up. It also marks a major turning point in my relationship with my mother. She had always been good to me, but she always seemed rather aloof. She had *hauteur*, probably because her children were so good in school. This whole facade crumbled when Dad died, perhaps because she realised how alone she was. Suddenly you could touch her, hug her and talk about anything under the sun. We had not done these things before. She stayed this approachable till the day she died, seven years later.

All good things, it seems, must end. In 1972, five years after my father's death, Field Marshall Idi Amin Dada in one fell swoop ended for ever this idyllic state. All people of Asian origin were expelled and our worlds turned upside down. Let me state clearly, we were expelled, not exiled. Exile hints at the possibility of return. Expulsion means for ever. And we went out with nothing. My eldest brother went to Canada; my mother, my second brother, my sister and I went to India. In the end we were the lucky ones. Many of my African friends were not.

In terms of becoming a person, of knowing my own identity, of finally confronting myself and all that sort of stuff, India was a haven. It was, however, disastrous academically because it's very difficult to get Indian qualifications recognised and accepted anywhere else in the world.

My brother and sister and I all ended up in medical school. When I look back I realise how incredibly lucky we were to have succeeded. In Delhi only 600 applicants made it to medicine, out of the 10,000 or so who applied. My brother and I ended up in Amritsar, in Punjab.

At college I realised that liking men was not the done thing socially. People did it, but you still had to get married. In Indian society, if you are not married, you do not exist. Your identity is subsumed by your family. You are always someone's son, someone's father, someone's husband. You are not an individual. Still, if you are a man, you can get away with many things. You get married, have a few children, then go ahead and do whatever you want, as long as you are discreet.

I myself had a wonderful time at college. I never wanted for sex. It's funny, you know: I could go up and talk to boys in my class and say, 'I think you are really cute. I'd like to go to bed with you!' I did this quite a few times. They'd either laugh it off or accept. There was always the realisation that you did what you liked, but you had to be quiet about it.

When I first went to medical school there was a big scandal. A senior student had been caught in bed, *in flagrante delicto*, with a junior student. The junior, who was drop-dead gorgeous, had transferred to our college from out of town. There were always rumours as to the reason for his transfer. Apparently he would get into trouble with men because he was so good-looking. It seems to be a curse to be young and good-looking, especially if you are inclined to accept the advances of men. Fortunately I have never had this trouble. I mean, I am attractive, but I am glad I was never considered good-looking in that sense, because I don't want to have to deal with all that shit. The older student was of course at fault. He spent a year in a mental institution on drugs and ECT. He came back a shattered man. It was a graphic lesson in what happens when you digress from the path set by society. In the meantime, there was this other scandal. A college girl was raped and buggered and left for dead. The senior student offered to marry her. This was accepted. She was tainted goods, you see. Who would marry a raped woman? Once he married, of course, the student was suddenly accepted back into the fold.

I had one long affair that lasted about five years. The man I loved gave me a lot of support and was very good to me. He looked after me and protected me, a foreigner in the land of my forefathers. But, in many ways, it was a very destructive relationship. It sapped my confidence and I was at the beck and call of this one person who was insanely jealous. I believe now that he treated me as he would treat his woman. And I let myself be treated so because the urge to touch, to be touched and loved was overpowering. Of course, I had a girlfriend for a while, but there was no excitement whatsoever. I could not wait to leave her and be in the arms of my lover. He is married now. I met him again in 1985, with my lover, Jeremy. I am sure he was a bit pissed off, perhaps because he sensed he had no control over me any more.

I also used to see this sweet West Indian student who was hopelessly in love with me. I used him for sex, and feel guilty about doing this. One night we were lying in bed and he asked, 'Do you think we are homosexuals?' I thought, 'If I say "Yes", then he may never come back.' So I lied and said, 'No. We're just having fun!' Poor kid. I hope he's well and someone is returning his affections.

In 1978 I finished my degree. Under the terms of my admission, I had to leave India or pay a substantial bond. Technically I was still considered a foreigner, albeit a refugee. I applied and got a job with Waikato Hospital in Hamilton. It took two years to organise the necessary paperwork to come here and a further five to convince the authorities that I was a *bona fide* refugee. I am now a New Zealand citizen.

I came here knowing subconsciously that I was a homosexual and was quite content with this. I thought I would probably end up getting married while continuing to carry on with men! Then one day I was reading the *Waikato Times*, and staring me in the face was an ad for the Taurus Society, a club for gay men. I thought, 'That's me!' You know how you suddenly shed a skin? You get a moment of illumination in your life, your brain suddenly expands, and you know 'That's it!', there is suddenly a legitimate word? Yes, I was gay.

Years before, in Uganda, when I was about 15, I went to see a movie with my eldest brother. It was called *Night After Night* and was about this debauched, decadent judge who used to dress up in drag at night and kill prostitutes because he thought women were vile temptresses. In one scene he is walking down this alleyway, tottering on his high heels, wig askew, and my brother nudged me and whispered, 'That's a homosexual.' I guess I was supposed to laugh, but I just froze and thought, 'Oh my God, that's me!' So when I saw this ad, again I thought, 'That's me!', but this time I was glad.

Fitting in at the Taurus Society was difficult, initially. I seemed to be the only Indian face around. But it was here that I met my lover Jeremy, and we lived together for nine years. It was here that I also took my first tentative steps towards a political consciousness and became involved in the Gay Rights of Waikato. And it was in Hamilton I found that sense of community again. Friday night was 'club night'. Our house was open, and people would drop in for food and then go off to the club, returning later for coffee and eats. A lot of younger gay men passed through, and I remember bringing some of them up to Auckland for the Gay Pride marches. One time I remember there were about 50 of us, and we marched down Queen Street, arms linked, pink bunting over us, walking behind this old jalopy blaring out Tom Robinson's song, 'Sing if you're glad to be gay'. That sense of community has, sadly, been sapped. For a while the HIV pandemic brought back a sense of togetherness and gave us a reason to build a community again, but that edge seems to have gone.

About two years into my relationship with Jeremy, my eldest brother rang me, and said, 'I've got a proposal for you.'

'What? Marriage?' I asked.

'Yes,' he replied.

'No,' I said. 'I am not getting married.'

'Why not?'

'I can't talk about this on the phone,' I said. 'I'll write you a letter.'

So I wrote and told him about Jeremy. We did not speak for six years. All my family know, but prefer not to talk about it. Yet, when I separated from Jeremy, they all rang to inquire if I was okay and if there was anything they could do.

My separation from Jeremy was another watershed. We parted amicably — I try to have good relationships with all my past lovers. After all, we have shared our lives together and have given one another some important moments. I was 35 when we went our separate ways. I was not too upset initially. I thought, 'Big deal, people separate all the time.' But I very quickly descended into this state of fugue and depression. Suddenly, I felt worthless. It took me four years to climb out of this hole.

It was right in the middle of this bleak period that a childhood friend turned up from England. We had not seen each other since 1971. Through him I rediscovered my past and my worth as an Indian man. I re-established my old connections and associations. Through this I discovered a deep, inner bedrock of solidity and strength which I could hold on to in times of distress. I am certain that my rediscovery of my Indian heritage saved me from death.

Part of my depression was engendered by the break-up

with Jeremy, and the rest by the sudden accumulation of all past losses. I grieved for the losses, separations, family break-ups, deaths and the loneliness that I had stoically endured since the expulsion from Uganda. Most people go to school, university and work if not in the same city, then in the same country. They can expect to meet friends and colleagues who shared their growing up. I did not have that. From 1972 onwards, I ceased to have a past. I had to go searching for it to find it. It wasn't until 1991 that I went to England and the USA and met the boys/men who had been part of my growing up. I remember walking into this pub in Harrow. I saw a man sitting there. He reminded me of a school friend we used to call Mosquito. I went up to him and said, 'Mosquito?'

He replied 'Ravinder?'

'Yes.'

He said, 'Before you say anything, tell me what you do.'

'I am a doctor,' I answered.

He started jumping up and down and shouting, 'See, I told you you would be a doctor!' And I thought, 'Fuck! Twenty-eight years later, here we are and all these people know me. This is what I've missed.'

But I am getting ahead of myself. In 1984 Jeremy and I had left Hamilton for Auckland, where I went into private practice and became a big-time HIV doctor. I joined the Auckland branch of the New Zealand AIDS Foundation and was elected to the board. In 1990, with my depression gathering, I quit everything. I sold up my surgery, my house, gave away my dog and left New Zealand.

This ended up being a two-year voyage of discovery. I travelled the world and rediscovered friends from my childhood. I met family I had not seen in years. I went back to Uganda and started healing my wounds of rejection. All my friends know that I'm gay. One of the school friends I stayed with in England said to me, 'When people love you, it does not matter who or what you are.' I was near to tears when he said that. And that was how it has been with all those old friends.

I came back to New Zealand in 1992 and tried to settle down. I was still celibate, having been so since 1988. I just could not bring myself to have sex with anybody. Then, again, one of those illuminations: this lovely man from Wellington opened up my doors of perception and led me to believe that I was whole again.

In November 1992 I attended a conference on HIV in New Delhi, India. Here I met my current lover, Rajnish. He came and visited with me last year. Being in India, and falling in love with an Indian, felt so right. I came back from Delhi an Indian gay man.

Regarding being a person of colour and being gay: you cannot separate the two, in that I cannot confront or look at my identity as a gay person without also looking at my identity as a person of colour. The two are inseparable. The Western social construct of what it means to be a gay man is very much a creation of Western culture and, as such, isn't inclusive or understanding of what it means to be gay in a non-Western culture.

Rajnish is the new breed of Indian gay, no longer content to be quiet and accept social dictates. With his help I am discovering the vibrant gay culture of India. I am discovering the immensely rich gay cultural heritage of the land of my forefathers.

W a y n e [1]

I was born in 1954, and was adopted out at 18 months of age. My birth mother had hoped to keep hold of me and the sister born after me — both of us had the same father — but back in those days there just wasn't the DPB or the social supports. So we were placed with the Sisters of Mercy in the St Joseph's Convent in Herne Bay, though not at the same time.

I was adopted, as was my brother, into a Catholic family. He and I sort of got on, but at times we used to fight quite badly. I started school at an Auckland convent and can remember being really inquisitive, always wanting to find out things. When I was about seven or eight I got hauled out in front of the whole school because the nuns caught me up on the altar, where I was looking for God, actually. I knew he was supposed to live in that little tabernacle and I wanted to see him, so I found the keys and unlocked this door and pulled open the curtain to find him.

I ended up being sent to a government residential school for naughty boys, really — a school for children who were a bit difficult to handle, which I was, looking back. I stayed there until I turned 12, when I started at a Catholic high school on the North Shore where Mum and Dad had bought

1: Wayne has chosen not to use his last name to protect his family's identity.

a business. They were working seven days a week.

During my first years at high school I started to experience questions around my own sexuality. I used to have sexual encounters with schoolmates, but it was a very unsafe environment to explore anything other than heterosexual sex. It was especially unsafe for me because I was a largish boy and I hated playing rugby, I hated playing cricket, I hated sports. If you didn't do any of those, and you weren't an achiever academically, then basically you were nothing. That was the whole philosophy of the school.

I was still really quite naughty. I used to jump out the window and knock off Mum and Dad's car late at night, and do things like this. Once I got caught pinching the car and driving around with a group of friends, and was taken to the Panmure police station. My parents were called up and told to come and get me. To this day Dad says that's the closest he's ever come to murder.

At age 16, after School Certificate, I left school and went to work as an apprentice cook at an island resort in the Hauraki Gulf. I signed on as an ATI-affiliated apprenticeship chef, earning $21.70 a week. I thought this was wonderful, my first taste of absolute freedom; previously, because of my unruly behaviour, I had never really been allowed to do much by myself. Mind you, looking back, some of my behaviour invited this degree of supervision. Little wonder my mother would take me to the school dances and collect me afterwards. Anyway, it was at work I met alcohol for the first time, and I started to drink a bit. After about nine or 10 months I moved into town and started in the kitchens of a city hotel.

At this stage — I was about 17 — I was still wearing boys' clothes. I started to go to the gay bars of the day — the Lily

Pond, which was the camp name of the men-only bar in the Great Northern Hotel at the bottom of Queen Street; the Snake Pit, a basement bar under the South Pacific; and the Bridgeway Tavern, also known as Ma Gleeson's. One time, I was sitting in the Lily Pond, and in walked my old high school phys. ed. instructor, a religious Brother. He had left the order and was now an out gay. I nearly fell over sideways. There was one gay club, the old Aquarius Club in Elliott Street, and a few gay-friendly clubs, like the Embers night-club around the back of High Street. I also liked to visit Mojo's night spot, in the days of Nicole Duvall, Lee Mercedes, Kerry and Felicé. I thought I was just wonderful, striding around town in boys' clothes with a huge poncho.

I had a few gay friends by now — not a hell of a lot. There was Bill, whose camp name was Sophie, and Tom who we called April. I was Ella. There were only a few of us, really, and we never felt that we belonged to the gay scene. We felt it was too cliquey and we thought we were too high camp for them. I can remember standing beside Tom in the middle of Queen Street, outside the Lily Pond, dressed in boys' clothes and twirling umbrellas at midday. Very high-camp.

At this time the top of Queen Street was a very dis-reputable area. The Rembrandt Hotel up there was a very wicked hotel where I had many an experience. Near the Rembrandt was the Westwind Cafe, a 24-hour coffee bar. I started going there quite a lot and it was at the Westwind that I started mixing with trans-gender people. Transsexuals primarily. As I said, I had never felt as if I fitted in as a gay man with other gay men. I never felt that I belonged, that I could score or anything like that. I ended up getting into drag, at 17 and a half.

It's tough now, doing drag, but it was really tough then.

It was a really outrageous thing in those days. And if you can imagine me, I'm six foot two, in stilettos and stuff . . .

I can still clearly remember the first night I ever went out in drag. I was put into drag by this queen — she's still alive — Sharelle. I can remember vividly what I wore. My mother actually gave me the money for my outfit, not knowing what it was for. I wore a rust-coloured, two-piece trousersuit, a long brown fall, and high cork shoes. It was very elegant, and I made quite a lot of money that first night, because I started working the streets.

At the time, I didn't see wearing drag as a way of avoiding being gay. I loved the fact I scored more when I wore drag. I had never really scored in boys' clothes, probably because I was incredibly overweight. But the minute I got into a dress, I scored.

It didn't take me long to leave the hotel kitchen. I didn't actually like the cooking industry and had only got involved in it, partly, because my mother wanted me to and it got me away from home.

Getting into drag brought two major changes to my life. No sooner did I get into drag than I started up working the streets for money. And, in order to cope with being in drag, which I found more difficult than being a boy, I ended up dropping pills.

I started flitting between Auckland and Wellington. If things got a bit hot, street-wise, in Auckland, I would go down to Wellington, where I first worked in Carmen's coffee shop in Vivian Street. This was in the days of Shelly, Rita and all those girls. Quite a few are dead now. The drag scene in Wellington appeared as cliquey as Auckland's, but I somehow managed to get my way in there. In fact everyone was really supportive. I waitressed for Carmen at the

Balcony, selling toasted sandwiches and coffee, and did the lighting at the Club Exotique. We were paid $10 a night.

But drag started to get tougher and tougher and I found it harder to keep up. Nicole Duvall invited me back to Auckland, to work with her at Tinkerbelle's, a new drag club opening above the old Cook Street Market, in what became the Ace of Clubs. I was the comic. I invited my parents to the opening night, which really would have been the first time my Mum and Dad had seen me in drag. They came along with my aunt and uncle. Oh, bizarre!

That job lasted for a while, until Tinkerbelle's got closed down. Even now, to this day, I don't know why it closed. I shifted across the street and became the comic at Mojo's. Remember Tiny Tina? A large blonde. This was after her reign there.

I was still doing the streets, still having lots of fun. One night I went over to the new gay boys' club, Backstage, down behind the Town Hall. I was quite out of it and they wouldn't let me in. They didn't admit out-of-it drag queens. I was so furious I pushed the club's front door right until it snapped off its hinges.

Mojo's closed, so I moved back to Wellington to work at Carmen's and the Club Exotique. About this time I started smoking a lot of dope, and in order to finance it — I don't know if I need to say all this, but it's been and gone and it's all history now — I started dealing a little bit of smoke on the side, in order to make ends meet.

Like I said, for me, drag was hard. I was now 20 years old, I was getting tired of being in drag. I'd been doing it for a few years, but didn't know how to escape it. Anyway, I rang up my old resort boss and got me and a drag friend, Dallas, jobs on the island as kitchenhands. Well, could you imagine us! Here's these two semi-butch drag queens turning up on the ferry and being greeted by the amazed hotel staff. They thought we were on together, which was far from the truth.

This job went well, for a while. My friend Tom — that's April — came over to work too. We used to have our few smokes and the odd pills and stuff, and we had some really funny experiences too. We used to get the Navy boats coming in and the Fisheries Protection launches. Quite often we all used to go on board and have a few drinks at the end of the night. One particular night I ended up with a Navy boy back in my unit. Well, he fell asleep, I fell asleep, and in the morning they couldn't find him. No one had any idea where he was. Just as they were getting ready to start dragging the harbour, he suddenly surfaces out of my room. I blushed for days. Now I can't even remember what his name was.

I turned 21 on the island. Mum and Dad had sent me money for a twenty-first birthday party, so I bought some Marque Vue, some smoke and some pills. April went and stole all my pills, got high, then fell in the swimming pool and knocked all her front teeth out. I got pretty wasted myself, and I can remember turning up for work the next day obviously in no condition to do anything.

One time April, Dallas and I wanted to go to Auckland to see the Eagles. We asked management for the time off. They refused, so the three of us walked out. We caught the ferry to Auckland but ended up not even making it to the concert. The next day I rang up and asked if April and me could come back, and they said yes — probably because we were good workers. When we worked, we worked.

Ever restless, I got bored and flew back to Wellington. By this stage I had started dabbling with injecting drugs, on and off. I stayed there for a little bit, still working the streets, but when I heard that the island managers had moved up north to run a country hotel I contacted them and asked for a job. Once again I was wanting to get out of drag, but was feeling very trapped, with nowhere to turn.

This was 1976. I was 22 years old, and I worked up north, saving my fare to Sydney. I was still in drag, but I bought myself a couple of boys' outfits because I was petrified of going to Sydney in drag. As it was, I walked through Customs in Sydney, and they pulled me to one side and opened my suitcase. Out fell all this women's gear and here's me in boys' clothes. They said, 'Who's this for?' and I said, 'Oh, it's for my sister.' So I got through.

In Sydney I stayed with some friends and I got into drag there. By now I'd basically been living full-time drag for five years, with the odd space in and out. In Sydney drag was a different kettle of fish altogether. Like, at that point, you could not wear drag down the street, else you'd be arrested on some charge — either offensive behaviour or a serious affront to public decency. Whenever you walked out your front door, you'd look right, look left, and run, so you wouldn't be arrested. You made sure you always had $100 in your pocket, because that $100 paid your bail for the night. The fear of arrest ruled drags' lives.

I started working in Kings Cross in the mid-'70s, when the Vietnam War had started to wind down. You still had the Yankee sailors coming into town, and I had many an unprotected encounter. Occasionally you'd use condoms, but nine times out of 10 all you were worried about was clap.

I was first arrested in the Cross sitting in a back bar of the Crest Hotel. I ended up in a cell in the Darlinghurst police station for the night. It was the most horrifying night of my life, because it was so foreign. I'd been arrested in New Zealand on and off, but over here I knew the system. In Sydney it was a totally new, totally foreign system.

Some time later a group of us — me, my friend Pania and two Australian queens — decided we'd all go into hospital together and have our busts done. Now I always said that I would never tamper with my body in any way — I always said that — but I went along with the whole flow of things. Having breasts meant making more money, so I ended up having them done. I don't know how the operation was paid for. To this day, I've never paid for it.

I ended up working in a sex club. I can't remember the name of it, it's down a back street. I used to pay X amount of dollars a night for protection and so much per trick.

At one stage I got arrested for unpaid offensive behaviour fines and was thrown into Long Bay Prison for six weeks. This was the most horrifying experience of my life. Here I am, in a man's prison, with these titties. I had to do favours in order to be looked after, which I really hated. But you had to do it to keep your head above water, to make your stay in prison as safe as possible. I was involved with one of the heavy pins in charge of the laundry.

By mid-1977 — I was 23 years old — I was injecting drugs, doing a bit of smack, a bit of speed, and I got into such a state of paranoia that a friend came up from Melbourne and took me back there to calm down. Melbourne was a lot safer for me, as a drag, because there wasn't a charge for walking on the streets as there was in Sydney. I started working the massage parlours, but kept injecting more drugs. What I'd do is, I'd swap from one habit to another habit, thinking I was knocking it on the head, but it was just a vicious circle.

I had platinum blonde hair at the time. I was living in

Balaclava with another New Zealand queen, Robyn, and an Australian called Samantha. We were doing very well. We had our lives. Okay, we were injecting drugs and dropping pills, but that was our life. We did those things to cope. To handle life.

I was working in this parlour out in Frankston when there was a knock on the door. There stood this guy, really quite nice-looking. He says, 'How much for the massage?' I gave him the full quote. Then he says, 'How much for sex?'

I thought, 'Well, he can't be a cop,' because I knew the police were not allowed to ask that. It's called entrapment. I gave him the whole works, and the next minute, they're in! The place just swarmed with cops. He'd caught me.

He says, 'Are you a man or a woman?'

'I've had the sex change, love,' I replied, so they charged me as a woman.

A few days later, the policeman who arrested me came around to my flat and said, 'Look, Ella, we've got to take you down to the police station to give you an internal. A check.'

I thought, 'Oh God! Fuck! That's all I need!' So I said, 'I'm not a girl. I've not had the operation, okay.'

I was charged with prostitution. At this time, everyone was going down for seven to eight months for that charge.

From here on out, things got really tough for me, emotionally. Before the case went to trial I moved into St Kilda and went back to working the streets. I was feeling very lonely, very vulnerable, like I didn't belong. I would wander the streets in the middle of the nights, looking for companionship. That companionship turned out to be sex, but that was the only sort of companionship I knew. By now I was using quite a lot of heroin. I overdosed several times in Melbourne, and I can remember one time I ended up in St Vincent's Hospital . . . no, it's not St Vincent's, I can't remember what the name of it was. But I don't even remember getting there.

One day I went to visit friends who lived nearby, and when we were walking back to my flat we heard fire engines.

'Hey, there's a fire!' I yelled. 'Hey let's go!' I have always had this thing about fire engines. I really like them. We ran into my street, only to find it was my flat that was on fire, and all my stuff was out on the front lawn, burnt. Fuck! I'd lost everything. I had nothing left. Only what I stood up in. I wasn't insured. (I am these days. I learnt my lesson.) I was really devastated.

I ended up staying with a New Zealand woman, a sex worker, and this is where more confusion came into my life. I ended up having a couple of sexual encounters with her. These were my first sexual experiences with a woman. I would have been 23. These fair put the shits up me, excuse the expression, because I thought, 'I've been living this way and now this has happened. Where am I? Who am I? What am I doing?' I thought, 'Fuck this, I'm off.' So, I shifted countries.

After my time in prison in Sydney, I said I'd never go back to prison in my life. As I said, everyone going down for the prostitution charge was getting seven to eight months. So I appeared, pleaded not guilty, and jumped bail and came to New Zealand. I went straight to Wellington and arrived with a raging heroin habit. There just wasn't any heroin around in Wellington at that time, so I was quite unwell for a few days. I managed to get enough smoke and pills to get me through it.

That August — we're talking 1978 — I was still taking

drugs, still on the streets, still in drag. One night a group of us went onto the ships in Wellington, and we went a little crazy. We were all out of it when we wandered into the ship's bar and found it empty. So we picked up the cashbox, a bit of silver and Christ knows what else, and got out onto the wharf. The next minute the police turn up. I said, 'I'll take the rap, girls. I'll take the rap.'

We started throwing all our ill-gotten gains over the side. Biff! Biff! Biff! But I thought, I'm not throwing this cashbox over the side, so I threw it up on the roof instead. Of course I was caught out, and I got charged for stealing a cashbox. It only had something ridiculous like 98 cents in it.

When I was taken down to the police office that night, down come all these charges from Australia. They'd done a fingerprint match. There was a swag of them and I thought, 'Oh no!' Luckily the New Zealand police didn't consider them extraditable offences and they had no impact on my local case, for which I was merely fined.

Always, somewhere along the line, something or somebody was watching over me, because when I look back I'm absolutely stunned that I didn't spend more time in prison. Okay, I got nabbed, but I never went down for anything major, which I could have done. It's so easy to make the wrong move, or the wrong man. I never did, and my lucky streak stuck with me all the way along.

In Wellington I'd met up with this other woman, Lee, who I'd known before I left for Australia. Lee and I formed a sexual relationship, which just blew me totally sky high, right out of the water. I was getting more confused than ever about me, who I was, where I was going. The more confused I became, the more and more substances I used. In September, Lee arranged to go into a treatment programme in the Bay of Plenty for her addiction. I rang up my friend Tom, who was actually working there at the time, to see if I could come too. Tom, who was the first person ever sent to this community by the court system, managed to get me in.

This is when my reform really started, in September 1978, aged 24 years old. Until this time, in all the years I'd injected drugs, I chose never to go onto a methadone programme. Only junkies did that, and I had convinced myself that I wasn't a junkie.

I still had my breast implants, and felt very self-conscious about them. I was put into the boys' dormitory, and I would always try to keep them covered. I remember someone screaming at me, saying, 'Don't try and cover them. No one's looking at them.' This made me feel about knee-high to a grasshopper. I actually had my implants removed in February the following year, in the local hospital. There was a lot of fear involved in removing my implants. This was a very big move for me, a very difficult decision to take. Ella had been my identity, my alter ego, for so many years. It was very difficult giving her up.

By the end of 1979 I was still in treatment and recovery. Lee had left and I became close friends with Anne. So close, in fact, that we ended up getting married, during Labour Weekend of 1982. I was 28 years old.

Anne and I left treatment totally drug and alcohol free, and went fruitpicking in Motueka. One day I was up a fruit tree and I said, 'I hate this,' so we moved to Christchurch, where we both worked as kitchenhands, before I bluffed my way into a truck-driving job.

The guy said, 'Do you know your way around Christchurch?'

I said, 'Yeah, I know how to get to Hornby, Papanui and

Sumner.' And I did — from going there on the bus. No other way. I drove a truck for five or six years.

During these years I started doing my Central Institute of Technology training in Drug and Alcohol Studies, and eventually Anne and I were invited to work at the Bay of Plenty treatment centre, which we did.

All this time I still had issues about my identity. Many a time, you know, I was still looking at guys, feeling very attracted to them. I hadn't felt safe enough to explore these issues while I was in treatment, where there was a very strong message that you could explore who you were, so long as you stayed within their boundaries.

During our seven years working in the Bay of Plenty Anne had our first child, and just after we left there, for Auckland, she had our second. Although settled in Auckland with my young family in our own home, I was finding that the internal questioning of my own sexuality was becoming even stronger. Where was I going? What was I doing?

Then, three years ago — I was 36 — I went to a conference in Melbourne. Going back to Australia was an overwhelming experience. It was like revisiting the past life of someone I used to be.

Just an aside to all this: because I had a history of so many arrests in Australia under so many different aliases, I thought it would be just my luck to get caught entering the country, now that everything's on the computer. So I was careful to take a whole stack of letters from employers and doctors about my reform, showing I was a changed person. I had all this information proving I had finished my own recovery and was a totally different person. But the Australians never asked to see it. Obviously I'm clean over there now.

Anyway, going back in Melbourne became a personal

journey of rediscovery — a rediscovering of me, who I was and what I wanted out of life. It was a very healing experience. A time when I accepted and said goodbye to the past and felt ready to venture on into the future.

This philosophical journey was very much an internal process. I didn't externalise it, I didn't discuss it with anyone. But from this point onwards I found it more and more difficult to stay within my marriage. I didn't rush anything. It actually took me two and a bit years of thinking and waiting before Anne and I separated. I remember starting every day thinking, 'Hey, what am I doing here? Why am I here?' To which I'd answer, 'For the children.' Then I'd say, 'That's a crappy reason.'

Despite the great degree of security that staying within my marriage offered me, I left it. Anne really helped and supported me by pushing the issue and, in opening the door for me to explore who and what I was, by giving me permission to leave — I'll always be grateful to her for that.

Leaving my family was the hardest thing I've ever done in my life. If the family had consisted of just me and Anne it would have been a lot easier to leave. But there were my children and, in a way, it would have been a lot easier to stay there for them. But I knew that my staying would be emotionally crippling for all of us. I gave the grounds for leaving as sexuality.

Despite the difficulty I found in taking this step, the minute I left the relationship I knew that I'd never return. I could no longer endure concealing my feelings, hiding them and trying to live someone else's life. I was trying as hard as I could to live the life of a heterosexual male. But inside I knew it was a lie — one I couldn't continue to live. Hiding from myself was becoming harder and harder and harder.

I'd already booked a whole lot of counselling sessions for myself, and on the way to my first session, I knew what I was going to have to say. That I was gay. I nearly couldn't face it. I nearly turned around. But I chose not to. I went down that road and I said, 'Hey, I'm gay, I'm frightened and I'm scared and I don't know where I'm going.' I walked into that first session feeling like a little slug and I walked out feeling like a giraffe, tall and very proud. This dramatic change came from the counsellor, who really affirmed my decision and my identity. This was the first external confirmation I'd had of the rightness of my philosophical journey, which had been until then very much an internal, isolated one. My first counselling session dispelled all my doubts. It truly affirmed for me, and made me really accept, that I'd done the right thing. From that point on, my life has been a journey forward.

I told the children a week before I left that Daddy was moving out. At first my son got really excited. 'Wow!' Because solo families were quite the norm in the area. But he came down to earth about an hour later. I remember him and I spending time in the back yard just holding each other, just talking and crying.

Once I made the decision that the relationship was going to be over and I was going to be moving out, everything seemed to fall into place. I picked up the paper, looking for a flat to rent, and the one and only place I looked at I got. I'm still living there. All the things I needed to furnish my flat just turned up somehow, too. I found a bed and table and chairs. Anne and I looked under the house together and sorted through our wedding presents and stores. There seemed to be some doubling up there, so I got more household stuff. Like I said, everything seemed to fall into place as if it was meant to be.

A friend helped me move out of the house and what I vividly remember about moving day is watching my daughter, who was about three. All I could see was this sad little face looking up at me. The kids came and stayed with me the first night and helped me unpack. That was very hard. They were supposed to visit with me every weekend, but for the next couple of weekends my daughter chose not to come. She stood there and said, 'I'm angry.' I thought it was great that she felt confident enough to let me know her feelings.

The relationship between me and Anne is pretty good now. We're slowly rediscovering one another. Naturally it gets strained at times, and that's really difficult, but you can't help that. Sometimes, when we meet, we're very civil, and other times we sit down and really talk. We share custody of the children, and there are no issues around access.

Having said that, the past few years have been a real struggle. Not so much of finding myself, because I knew, I actually knew, who I was. What I've been trying to do since moving out is to re-establish myself within and re-connect myself to the gay community and with people from my past. I've discovered that the gay community is nothing like it was way back in 1971. It's very spread out now. It's more a collection of communities than just one community.

I'm now a counsellor for a gay community group. Five years ago I set myself the goal that, within five years, I would be working within the area of gay-related health issues. I heard about my current job just after leaving my family and thought, 'Should I apply? Do I really need another change in my life right now?' But I felt increasingly disempowered where I was then working. These feelings weren't anything to do with being gay. Rather, after five years there, I didn't see much opportunity for advancement. So I applied and got the new job I really wanted, achieving my goal in four and three-quarter years.

I really enjoy working here because the people who walk in the front door primarily want to do something. That's the big difference from my previous counselling position, where the people I saw were quite often sent to me by the courts. They hadn't chosen to come, whereas people choose to walk in here, seeking help with their anger, their hurt, their grief, their shame, their guilt, their relationship.

Ever since I started to work with gay men I've been blooming. I know I've been blooming. I feel good. I'm alone, I live alone, but I'm getting to the point now where I want to move from that space into a relationship with someone.

Looking back over this brief history, I realise there's a lot that I've missed out. There's a whole lot more stuff to talk about, especially about the prejudice I encountered first as a gay male and a Roman Catholic, and second when you're living that life in drag: how it feels having to cope with walking down the street and being laughed at by strangers; about being laughed at by the police here in Auckland; about being beaten up by the police in Sydney for resisting arrest. One way to cope with this constant prejudice is to build your own defence mechanism, learning to abuse others before they abuse you. You know, learning to yell, 'Hey! What are you looking at?'

As I said earlier, gay life is different these days from what it was in the '70s. It used to be very high camp — that's the way I look at it. High camp was a way of acting, doing lots of things with the hands. We had camp names and acted very *femme*. It was like acting. It was theatrical.

Back then gay life was very much on the outer. It's totally different now; it's much more accepted. In some respects I think it's good that gays are being mainstreamed, if you want to describe it like that. But at the same time we've lost that sense of being a tiny little community. We've spread out. However, if the trend towards gay-bashing increases, as it has in Sydney, this aggression might pull the various gay communities back together. A common cause seems to bring people together. In Sydney gays and lesbians patrol their streets and keep an eye on gay beats. I don't know if that'll happen here or not.

In New Zealand the effects of the HIV virus are pulling our community together. People tend to feel the pull of community protection and self-preservation when HIV hits someone in their immediate circle. Earlier this year, after a guy died of AIDS, I counselled a number of his friends who'd never been tested. Suddenly HIV was their business.

I've lost lots of friends to HIV. I've also lost many friends to substance abuse and related issues, whether they've ODed, fallen out of cars, been bashed, knocked over or murdered. I've had a lot of pain over the years. A lot of heartache. A lot of struggles. But for some unknown, Godforsaken reason, I don't know why, I'm still here. Looking back at friends who haven't made it, I often think, 'There but for the grace of God go I.'

It was the connection between injecting drug use and HIV, and also losing my friends, that got me interested in working in this area of health education. This is where I feel I very much belong, working inside the gay community. It's like I've finally come home and put the icing on the cake. That's how it feels for me. It's a real power, a sense of internal power.

Neville Wright

G o back to 1950, 6 March. It's 7.30 in the evening in Te Puke, which is about 30 kilometres from Tauranga. That's when, and where, I was born. Then in 1951 my sister Maureen was born. The following year my mother had a miscarriage. Then, in January 1954, my other sister Susan was born. So there were three of us, two girls and a boy. Yes, well . . .

We lived out on a farm, on Te Matai Road, about 10 kilometres from Te Puke. It may not sound a long way out, but we were on a loose metal road, not easy to drive. In those days, even the road between Te Puke and Rotorua was loose metal. Mum and Dad had a brand new little Austin car and you felt every bump and ridge in the road.

We lived, and Dad worked, on a dairy farm. Dad worked for wages. He wasn't even a share milker. To be honest, he was working for Mum's parents. When I was about five years old, my grandparents decided to sell the farm and take a world trip on the proceeds. This left Mum and Dad without a home or an income. Luckily, Dad found a job on another farm a kilometre down Te Matai Road.

Dad couldn't understand how his in-laws could sell up their farm and spend all their money on an overseas trip, forcing him, Mum and their grandchildren to look for a new home and a new job. He felt they should have at least helped him and Mum into a better position, so they wouldn't have to struggle. He became quite bitter about it, but Mum, even if she agreed with him, never criticised them. In fact she often used to say, 'If they wanted to sell the farm and spend all their money on a world trip, it's their business. That's what they wanted and that's what they got.' I suppose you don't think ill of your parents.

So anyway, we moved to this horrendous little house right by the roadside, with no shelter from the noise of the cars and trucks, or from the dust, which covered absolutely everything in summer. When we went blackberrying, you never picked the ones that were covered in dust. That's how bad it was. There was no shelter from the wind, which would blow so hard the house shook. We stayed there for six years until Mum and Dad went sharemilking, when I was about 11.

Growing up, we all got on quite well as a family, although my father was a fairly distant person. It's not that he wasn't interested in us kids. Rather, he didn't really know how to relate to his own children. He was always out-going and great mates with everyone else, like my cousins, who were about my age, or the neighbours' kids, but distant with us and with Mum. Somehow, I don't think we were given the treatment we deserved.

Not that we saw much of him. Being a farmer, he was hardly ever home. When we got up in the morning, he was already gone and milking the cows. When we came home from school he was doing the afternoon milking or cleaning up or something, and didn't come in — this is when we were small — until just about our bed time. On weekends, if he wasn't feeding out or something, he'd only be home in the afternoon. Then it'd be a quick mow of the lawns or tinkering under the bonnet of the car — things which didn't exactly excite me. The one time he did something for us was putting up a basketball hoop for the girls. I can't remember him ever doing something for me.

It wasn't for years and years, in fact not until I left home, that Dad and I had more to do with each other and I grew to understand him a bit better. Now we have a reasonably good relationship, probably because I accept him for what he is. I don't try to change him any more: that was what tended to cause all sorts of arguments. Especially when I got into my teens I used to say, 'You should do this,' or 'You should do that.' I was frustrated and irritated when Dad did things which I didn't think were right. So I'd say something and Dad would just say, 'Yeah! Yeah!' and go his own way.

See, my mother and father are very placid people. They never argued. Hard to imagine, I know, but if Mum and Dad did argue, it was done so quietly that I was unaware anything was amiss. They must have had differing points of view at times, but they never fought or argued, which was really quite pleasing. Similarly, Dad couldn't stand it when us kids were naughty and misbehaved. He used to just disappear.

Mum's parents, however, fought and argued and hit each other. It was a bit horrifying for us, as small children, to see our grandparents fighting and hitting one another. They had 'plenty of go', I suppose you could say. A very out-going couple, they were keen on local politics and were involved in the start-up of the Social Credit Party in Tauranga .

With Dad away most of the day, my life was dominated by women: Mum, my sisters and my mother's mother, who had a lot to say for herself. Her name was Jean Frost, and she'd been a teacher. She was an amazing woman, just so intelligent. Every day she picked up the newspaper and did the crossword in less than five minutes. I loved her and we always had a very strong relationship.

Life was so different in the '50s. Wives didn't work on the farm. Women didn't work, full stop. You only ever went to town on a Tuesday and a Friday. Mum and Dad would go on a Tuesday to buy the food and whatever else was needed, and we all went in on Friday, late night. This went on, as regular as anything, for years. You grew your own vegetables. You had an orchard, but occasionally you bought the odd bit of fruit. You killed your own animals and shared the meat with the boss's family. The boss had a son and two daughters too, a few years older than me. We got on quite well. They were allowed to do more things on the farm than we were. Dad didn't like us wandering around because the boss worried we'd leave all the gates open or something.

I had the wanderlust from a very early age. Even at the age of four I'd go on walkettes around the place. I'd wander down the road and get into culverts. I'd climb trees and go into deep dark areas of bush. I quite enjoyed doing this sort of thing. Mum used to get a bit concerned about where I was. I wasn't really into playing with my sisters. They liked to draw and do those sorts of 'inside' things, whereas I preferred to go outside and explore. I'd look at plants, chase butterflies, gather insects in jars and taste flowers.

I've always had an interest in nature. Even from the age of four I was trying to grow a garden, and investigating plants and animals generally. I would find birds' nests and bring home little birds. And if we found anything — on a farm you're always finding the odd bird or stressed-out animal after a wet or windy spell — we'd bring it home and put it in front of the fire and try to revive it. I had a quite good success rate, but I can't say I ever had much success in raising baby birds. I was always much too kind with them. I'd over-feed them, then they'd die stuffed.

My first year at school, in 1955, I was a very dependent child, always wanting someone to take care of me. My very first day there was horrendous. Dad's boss's daughter Anne, who was two years older than me, was told to look after me. She ended up having to give me her lunch because mine was stolen.

In those days you did as you were told, and one of the things I had to do was learn to write with my right hand. This rule was discarded a couple of years later, so I was one of the last ones who was forced to do it. Still, in other ways school did provide an outlet for your natural instincts. Every Friday afternoon, in the primers, we were allowed to dress up in drag. We'd get the boxes out and there were all these old dresses and high heels. That was my favourite time. I'd rush to get the box out and dress up in these high heels and chiffon dresses. They were far too long, of course, so in order to walk I had to haul them up around my neck. I loved it.

Friday was also the day we'd see the big boys, who'd come in from country schools for technical training. I was quite taken with them — they could only have been 11 or 12 themselves — and I loved to show off in front of them. A few years later I actually had a classroom right next to the technical class. Many a time I'd spend morning break or lunchtime looking out the window and literally perving on these older boys. I was about eight or nine. I didn't know about sex, but I was definitely interested. I don't know what I thought I was doing. It was just a desire to be with spunky men, I guess.

At seven I had a little friend, the caretaker's son, who lived right beside the prefab where we waited for the school bus every afternoon after all the other kids had gone. He used to take me under the prefab, where we would play with each other's tiny stiff dickies. I definitely did not encourage it. It was all his doing. He knew where to go. I didn't. It wasn't something I was madly keen on. It wasn't like I was waiting desperately for the next day, for it to happen again.

Then, when I got on the bus, I was regularly abused by this big boy, about six years older than me. He was in form three. He used to beckon me down the back of the bus, where he'd be sitting in his school shorts, with his legs open. I remember his hairy legs, so obviously he was developing. He'd make me rub him. I had to get on my knees, facing him, my face right at his crotch, and masturbate him. Wank him off in the back of the bus. Maybe I had to rub my nose and my head in there too, I'm not certain. This happened on a regular basis. Nobody noticed.

You may think, 'How did I feel?' I thought it was a bit strange and all a bit odd. There was nothing in it for me. He told me to tell nobody, so I didn't, until years later when I thought it was rather hilarious. Actually, he grew up to became a lawyer and, as far as I know, has never married.

He turned up elsewhere in my life, too, in Sunday school, of all places. For two or three years Mum sent us to Presbyterian Sunday school, until one day my sisters and I decided that, instead of waiting for the Reverend to give us a lift to the little country church up the road, we'd hide in the bushes until he'd gone past. For a few weeks we'd hide, then come out and play once he'd gone by. When we thought the church service was over, we'd go home.

One day Mum was in conversation with the Reverend. He commented that he hadn't seen us for a while. Mum said we'd been going regularly, but of course we hadn't. We were forced to confess our truanting.

Part of the reason I didn't want to go to Sunday school was because the boy from the back of the bus also went, with his family. There I would be, all dressed up in my Sunday best, feeling so embarrassed because, although I was only small, I had enough savvy to realise what he made me do wasn't right. He would look at me and give me a smirky, 'I know' smile. I was a bit frightened of him. It was all right in the back of the bus, because it was only a short journey home and then I was free. But at Sunday school I had no Mum and Dad nearby, just my sisters, and I was supposedly protecting them. He was much older and manipulative, and I didn't know what he might do. I feared him. I did. That's one of the reasons I didn't want to go back to Sunday school, and I must have persuaded my parents, who weren't at all religious either, to let us stay home.

Later on, of course, I went through a stage in my teens when I became very religious. I wouldn't swear. I believed everything was God-given and homosexuality was immoral. It was a denial thing, which lasted two or three years, during which I got terribly fat. I ate a tremendous amount of food. I had a minor psychological problem trying to cope with being gay, and this came to a head around the age of 15.

Meantime, also waiting for the bus was another boy about my age, who was rather stupid but very nice-looking. I would manipulate him into playing husband and wife with me. Of course he was the husband and I was the wife. But by God, I wore the pants in that relationship, getting him to do this, that and the other! In fact, even at that age, at six and seven, there was definitely a sexual undertone to our play. I had a natural sort of — I don't know — drive to be with boys and play the wife role, although I have never, ever wanted to be a woman.

Things changed around eight or nine when I picked up with this girl. She and I became the best of buddies. It was more than a simple friendship. We were literally obsessed with one another. We sought each other out every moment of the day, whenever we had the chance. She had big blue eyes. Her straight, very blonde hair was cut extremely short. She had a gruff voice and a boyish manner. I'd drag her along to watch the tech boys with me. I don't think she was the slightest bit interested in them, but I was, so she had no choice. It got to the point where she had no girlfriends and I had no boyfriends. It became such an obsession that the school became concerned and our parents became concerned, and put an end to the relationship.

The following year, 1960, when I turned 10, I moved to a new school. Here I formed quite an unusual relationship with another boy. There was never any sex involved, except he liked kissing me frequently. He also liked keeping me under his control. I was his friend but I was also his slave, in a way. He was definitely stronger than I was. But I don't think he could cope with his homosexuality, because when we moved up to secondary school we tended to go our own ways. We had different circles of friends. He didn't stay in Te Puke when he reached his adulthood. Years later I heard he'd committed suicide, at the age of 31. Quite sad.

Things changed during these final terms at primary school and the first terms at secondary. These were those adolescent growth days — finding pubic hairs growing, and hair appearing under your arms. It was also the time when a little bit of bullying started, and I began to realise that something was amiss, because people were starting to point out differences between me and everyone else. They would comment on the way I used to walk and wobble my arse. They'd call me a Susie. 'Oh, you're a real Susie today,' they'd say. Or a sissy, or a girlie, or something. Those were the terms that were used in those times.

At the end of the third form I had my appendix out and I couldn't do any swimming. So, while the rest of the class had swimming, I had to sit by the pool with this other boy, who was also not allowed to swim for some reason. He was very nice-looking and quite well developed. I'd follow him around and we'd talk about things. We got to talking about wanking. I'd just got to the stage when I was about to do this myself — around 13, just about 14 — and, after he'd described what it was like, I had to go home and find out, didn't I? That was my first experience with playing with myself. Of course, I had this sort of moral scruple that masturbation was bad for you. We hadn't had what I would call a religious upbringing, but my grandmother was very religious and she'd always read us stories from the Bible and given us books of religious stories. I must have picked up these moral scruples from her.

On the home front, it was about this time that Mum and Dad started to find their feet financially. They moved into a share-milking position, which is quite a different situation from working for wages. Once again we moved down Te Matai Road, the road we'd always lived on, to a new farm about six kilometres from town.

Now Dad had to run the place and we all helped out. Mum used to milk the cows. I used to have to get up early, prepare breakfast for me and my sisters, then go to school.

When we came home in the afternoon, around four o'clock, we'd have a quick bite to eat, then go and help Mum and Dad in the cow shed. At various times we had to feed the calves, feed out the ensilage and the hay, that sort of thing. I'd help Dad on the weekends to give Mum a bit of a break. I was involved in hay making until, unfortunately, I started to get hay fever in a pretty ghastly way, and couldn't work. This was very hard on my father, because labour was costly and he wanted it as cheap as possible — in other words, free. To his way of thinking, I was a boy, I was physically healthy, so I should be working. I'd try to help, of course, but my nose would start streaming, my eyes and face would swell, and I'd have to go to bed. Eventually it got so bad I had to go to the doctor, who gave me anti-histamine pills. These dried out my sinuses but they also made me so headachey and lethargic that I couldn't do anything. I used to feel like a great blob and, of course, I was developing into a big blob, because I was quite chubby.

I can remember the very moment I realised that I was homosexual. I was in the fourth form and I was coming out of class one day — either French or Latin. My God. It all comes back. From memory it was summer. I was with this nice straight boy, Graham, whom I really liked, and a couple of his friends. We all came out of the classroom. There was nobody else in the hallway. Graham turned to me and said, 'D'you know, Neville, what a homosexual is?'

'No,' I said.

He said, 'It's when a man loves another man.' Not, 'when a man has sex with another man,' because in those days you didn't use those words. Everyone was far too polite.

'It's when a man loves another man,' he said, and I thought, 'That's me.' It was like a flash.

'That's what I am,' I said, and things fell into place.

I'd been wondering, because for the few months previous to this, some of us boys had taken to sitting on the terraces by the swimming pool, near the girls' changing shed. When the girls came out, the boys would get all excited. They'd discuss the girls and they'd say, 'Neville, don't you think . . . blah, blah, blah . . . this one's beautiful . . . this one's got shapely . . .?' I didn't know what the hell they were talking about. I couldn't wait to flee. I was not the slightest bit interested. But when the head boy went past . . . Well! I had two or three other favourites. There were these fraternal twins who were both super-looking, and when they walked up and down the swimming pool — oh, I just swooned!

Once I became aware of myself and realised I was gay — though, of course that wasn't the word we used, it was homosexuality — I became very concerned about being different. I was different in other ways too. I wasn't able to relate to the things boys did, like sport. It just didn't interest me.

The funny thing is, even in a small town like Te Puke, I met up with two other gay boys. One was tall and slim, a Pakeha; the other was a chubby Maori boy, about my height and weight. Strange as it may seem, we'd talk about sex all day but never discuss our own sexuality. The three of us were the campest things in school. We couldn't have been anything else but camp. We weren't in the same classes — I was in the top stream and they weren't — but every morning interval and lunchtime we got together because we had this affinity with one another. We definitely had empathy. Even though we were quite unsuited in many other ways — I mean, we couldn't talk to each other on the same level on many topics — we had this feeling that we had to stick together and support one another. We used to go around and look at the boys. And we'd sit down together and my Maori friend would cross his legs and wave his hands and tell us which boy had a big prick by looking at the bulge in his pants. We kept this friendship until they left school, a couple of years before me.

My parents, being racist, disapproved of my friendship with a Maori. They were very much against it. This was very hurtful and hard to deal with. In those days country people had very conservative, extremely narrow points of view. My parents would probably have been just as upset if I'd been interested in a heterosexual relationship with a Maori girl. It was the way things were then, even in the mid-'60s, which was just awful.

I wasn't racist. Some of the greatest shrieks I had at school were with the Maori girls, who used to send me up gutless because I was such a camp thing. I wasn't camp intentionally, it was just me. And they picked it up and teased me about it. They'd say, 'Your arse is bigger than mine,' because I was getting a bit chubby.

Another relationship that was also nipped in the bud, or hit on the head, and smartly too, because of my parents' disapproval, was a friendship with a rather butch boy who quite liked me. Oh, I did fancy him. But just as we started to get to know each other, my parents made me break it off because, even though he was a Pakeha, he came from a very low socio-economic area in town and his mother was considered to be a 'you know what'. I wanted to be accepted by my parents and all the rest of it, so I probably said something like, 'My parents don't like my being friends with you.' It's a bit sad for a teenager to be pressured into conforming to such a narrow social circle.

By the fifth form, at the age of 15, I had a minor psychological problem. I knew what I was, homosexual, and I was denying it. I didn't want anything to do with homosexuality, and I started to eat. I ate myself sick. I got very stressed, and I'd go to bed at night and I'd cry and cry and cry for hours. I couldn't sleep. This made Mum stressed. Eventually she decided to take me to the doctor. There I am, 15 years old, totally naive. Nowadays most 15-year-olds are independent, sophisticated and quite worldly. They carry themselves really well. I was in a terrible state.

The doctor sat me down. 'You know, Neville,' he said, 'you know what they say about fat people?' He was trying to say that fat people are not always happy. 'When you're fat you feel that no one loves you and you feel that you're ugly.'

The whole time I was expecting him to say something about my homosexuality. I was waiting for him to say it. I thought my homosexuality was so obvious, everyone could see it. To me, the reason for my unhappiness was completely obvious. 'I know why I'm like this,' I was thinking. 'I know why I'm upset. It's because I'm homosexual and there's nobody else like that out there. I must be the only one.'

But because I couldn't say what I was worried about, the doctor wasn't any help, basically. I continued to have palpitations and panic attacks. I spent the next year worrying that I had heart disease. I'd wake up at night, anxious that I didn't feel well. I didn't feel safe. I became extremely fat and had to have special clothes made. I couldn't wear ordinary clothes any more.

Looking back, I find it almost incomprehensible that I couldn't connect my sexual orientation with the sexual orientation of my two gay school friends. Why couldn't I connect the fact that they were gay too? Why couldn't we three talk about it? After all, though we never talked about being gay, we spent all our time talking about the other boys and discussing which one was the nicest-looking. One day they rushed up to me, very excited because two boys had gone into the boys' toilet together and locked the door behind them. We knew exactly what was happening. We just knew what was going on in that toilet, but we never said what it was out loud.

Here I am today, a long-time secondary school teacher, and I've never seen any of these things happening at school, ever. Obviously they must go on, but I've never seen them. The teachers never do. These kids are much too shrewd. They know where to do these things without the teachers knowing.

A year later, in sixth form, in August, I got the flu. In fact it was something worse than the flu, it was a real fever. I had this very high temperature, 41 or 42 degrees. I was delirious for a couple of days. I lost heaps of weight in a week. The weight just burnt off me. A couple of weeks later, when I recovered enough to get up and get dressed, I discovered all my old clothes were too big and I could once again fit into normal-sized clothing. I felt like I had changed back into a normal person again.

Something had changed within me as well. This brain fever had altered my whole attitude to life. I accepted who I was and what I was. I accepted the fact that I was homosexual. Even though I still thought there was no one else like me in the world, I felt happier. I went back to school and back to study. I wanted to get a university Bursary, so I started to work very hard at my school work. Out of our class of 12 at Te Puke High, nearly all of us got A or B

Bursaries.

I left Te Puke for university in February 1968. I was 17. I had never been away from home before in my entire life, except for one week at my grandparents' house in Mt Maunganui. When Mum and Dad took me to get the Auckland bus, Mum and I cried at this final break. Even though it was a totally frightening prospect, I knew I had to leave and find my own place in the world. I knew there was no place for people like me in Te Puke.

On my first day at university, at my very first lecture, I met Wayne, who immediately became a very good friend. Not a lover, but a friend. He and I were both gay, and though we hadn't come out yet, we had an instant rapport. He had a circle of friends a couple years older than us who, it turned out, were gay too. Through his friends we were suddenly thrown into this whole gay world: the 'men only' bar at the Great Northern Hotel, the Snake Pit bar underneath the South Pacific Hotel, the Shakespeare Hotel and the Aquarius Club, where you knocked on the door and someone checked you out through a peep-hole before you were allowed in. So we got to know the scene and I got involved in my first relationship, which lasted six weeks. My second, which started the next year, lasted 14 years, on and off.

Clive and I were not the ideal couple. We'd argue. He could be quite violent. We separated several times. Once I fled to England, but Clive followed me four months later and persuaded me to get back together. During our fourteen years together we had two or three really good years here and there, interspersed with some fairly dreadful ones. I was foolish to stay with him for so long, and now wish I'd made a clean break from him earlier on. If I'd done so, my life might have had a different direction.

I believe that there's a person for everyone, and either you meet them in this lifetime or you don't. Since Clive, I've had a few relationships but nothing's worked out. My nature is such that I'd like to be in a permanent relationship, but I've set my mind to the fact that I might not find the right person. Either it happens or it doesn't. I'm not spending all my spare time looking for Mr Right. That search for romance has lost the desperate urgency it once had. I'd hate to be young again and have all those youthful emotions.

The one constant in my life has been my teaching career. I got into teaching because I saw how well other university students lived off their teachers' college salary while I was washing dishes until one in the morning for half the money, to pay my way through university. So I signed on as a trainee secondary school teacher. I started teaching in 1974 and am at the same school 20 years later. I've outlived numerous headmasters. My job has changed so much over the years, from teaching geography to teaching biology and horticulture. I run my own department. Being part of the school for so long, I'm an institution. I don't hide who I am.

Chris Carter

I was born on 4 May 1952 to Joe and Maureen Carter, in Panmure, Auckland. I'm the middle child in a family of three, having an elder brother and a younger sister. Dad was a truck driver, Mum a machinist. Both come from strong Irish Catholic families. Dad is descended from Fencible settlers who arrived in Panmure in 1847. He had 13 brothers and sisters; Mum was one of nine children.

I had a traditional Irish Catholic convent primary school education at St Patrick's Convent School in Panmure. Although I didn't think so at the time, I must have been fairly intelligent because I used to win prizes. Every year I won the Christian doctrine prize because, I think, I have good retentive memory, and Christian doctrine in the Catholic Church was the rote learning of set articles of faith, which had to recited at the appropriate point. Questions and responses such as 'Who is God?', 'God is an infinite being' were typical. The good Sisters were always telling my mother they were sure I was going to be a priest!

I was the nuns' 'chook boy'. When I was a baby, my mother says, the only way she could pacify me was to push my pram down near the hen house where I could look at the hens. I clearly became imprinted on poultry at a very early age, and when I went to the convent school I showed an abnormal and great interest in the nuns' hens. From New Entrants onwards, I would be found staring at the chickens whenever I could. The Panmure priest, Father Gardiner, also had hens, and I was put in charge of them too. Every night I fed the fowls and took the eggs to the convent. Still today my hobby is keeping old-fashioned breeds of chickens.

At primary school I felt valued and successful. However, things changed dramatically at the end of standard four when I left Panmure and began seven very unhappy years at St Peter's, a Christian Brothers secondary school in Newmarket.

I was an excitable and precocious child. I don't know if this is a feature of being gay, but I don't think so. I think I was just a lively child. I arrived at the big boys' school good at school work, and at talking, but not good at sport. The Brothers maintained discipline with the strap. From the first day in form one I was strapped almost daily, mostly for talking at the wrong time. I had a very unhappy first year. In fact I ran away. My mother was sent for and told that if I didn't behave I would be expelled — a remarkable event for an otherwise obedient boy. That night I got a good hiding — unusual because my parents weren't at all aggressive, but I had shamed the family. After a while I simply adjusted to St Peter's but was never very happy there.

I didn't realise that I was different from most of the other boys until third form, when puberty set in and sexual awakening happened. I had already learned from the Brothers' Christian doctrine lessons about the evils of masturbation and homosexuality. Our form one teacher, Brother Mason, told us, 'When you go to sleep at night, boys, you must keep your arms above your chest.' I thought, 'What an incredibly uncomfortable way to go to sleep.' I was a very innocent 12-year-old. I had no idea what he was talking about, or about masturbation. I must have come across the actual words masturbation and homosexuality later on, probably in my reading. I enjoyed reading very much.

In the third form I, like 99 per cent of my classmates, started masturbating. This was difficult to cope with because the Brothers told us it was a mortal sin. I tried to rationalise out the desire to do it with the guilt felt afterwards. The Catholic concept of penance was strongly ingrained in my Irish genes. If anything bad ever happened, I immediately believed it was punishment for my lustful thoughts about other boys. I felt any misfortune that befell me well deserved for my lustful urges.

I can recall the very instant that I knew I was gay. It happened in a flash. I was sitting in class, in the first week of the third term of my third form year. I looked at the boy sitting just in front of me — his name was Patrick — and I thought, 'I'd like to give him a kiss.' That was the sole sexual thought. Quite innocent, really. The moment I had that thought, I followed it up with another: 'Oh, I must be homosexual.' As soon as I said the word homosexual inside my head, it was like an instantaneous flash, and I knew it was true. Of course, I said, 'Oh no! I can't be,' but I knew it was true. From that moment of staring at Patrick and thinking I'd like to give him a kiss, I knew that I must be a homosexual. This became my guilty secret. I said prayers at night that it would go away, and spent a number of years racked with guilt.

The other thought that was strong in my head on the day of revelation (if we can call it that) was: what would my mother and father say if they found out? Many gay men and women face this thought when they realise they are gay.

Talking to friends, I've discovered we all had this fear of parental rejection. As dependent children, our parents are usually the most important people in our lives. Our whole world focuses around them, and their opinions are very important.

In 1971 I finished seventh form and left St Peter's to pursue two part-time education courses: one at Epsom Teachers' College, to become a school teacher; the other, at Auckland University, was an arts degree in English and History. University was the most liberating thing that ever happened to me. I loved it. Freedom at last!

At university, for the first time, I met openly gay people. I had mixed with a group of gay friends at St Peter's, but none of us ever said we were gay. Eight of us, in my sixth form class, later came out as gay. We gravitated to each other and, thinking back, we were all incredibly outrageous and naughty. We used to talk about how nice-looking other boys were, and wondered if they were gay or not. One of us used to fantasise about getting pregnant to the captain of the First Fifteen. Whenever he said this we'd laugh and think how shocking and outrageous, but we loved it. However, we weren't sufficiently liberated or knowledgeable, nor did we have the courage, to say, 'Well, you know, I'm one. I'm gay.' I never had a sexual relationship with any of them. We were just good school friends. The following year, at university, we finally came out to each other.

At university I met Nat, a second-year student, who was gay. Although we didn't have a sexual relationship, we became really close, very good friends. Nat was out and had discovered the Shakespeare, then Auckland's gay bar. So off the St Peter's crowd went to the Shakespeare and we had a great time. We all felt very comfortable, and here I started to meet other gay boys who did become sexual partners.

At the start of the university year in 1972 Nat, myself and a friend from training college, Nigel Baumber, attended the first Gay Liberation meeting ever held in New Zealand, arranged by Ngahuia Volkerling. So I was a political activist from the very beginning. After that first meeting we had the first gay demonstration in New Zealand, in Albert Park. There we were, this little group of intrepid gays, standing around the statue of Queen Victoria, holding up signs that said 'Gay Pride' and 'Gay Rights'. People gawked at us and it was all a bit exciting and a bit scary. This was my first public declaration of my sexuality, and it was quite difficult. I was still living at home, and still hadn't discussed being gay with Mum and Dad.

How did my parents find out I was gay? Actually I was outed by one of my friends from our St Peter's set. There was a complicated series of events — we had some sort of row, which resulted in him ringing up my parents and saying that Chris's membership card to the Gay Liberation Society was ready. It was just an awful thing to do, and I was very angry and very upset. But in a way it had its positive side, in that it was the catalyst that got everything out into the open.

That night, totally unsuspecting, I arrived home and my mother said, 'We got this phone call,' and explained what had happened. There was a terrible scene. I broke down and burst into tears and said, 'Yes it's true. I'm gay and it's all your fault!' I'm not sure how it was their fault, but as a teenager you say terrible, dreadful things to your parents, especially when you're anguished and fraught with emotion. Mum and I were in tears, and Dad was in a terrible mood.

My parents thought I should see a counsellor but I refused.

I've always been very stubborn and strong-willed. I insisted that there was nothing wrong with me, and promptly moved into a flat with my boyfriend, Alan. After a while, when the relationship with Alan broke up, I moved back home and saved up for a four-month holiday in the United States, taken during my holidays.

Home from the States, I got a part-time job in Cornwall Park Hospital where, 21 years ago, I met Peter, my partner, the love of my life. He was 16 and in the sixth form at Kelston Boys. I was 20 and in my second year at varsity. It was lust at first sight which very quickly became love at second sight. At the end of the holidays Peter and I went to Europe for an extended holiday. He was extraordinarily young — he still hadn't turned 17. We bought a car and spent four months camping on our own. This very significant step in our relationship forced us to adjust to each other at a very young age. We did this very successfully, discovering we had an enormous amount in common. We grew very close and have never been separated since.

Peter and I have always lived openly gay lives. We've never pretended to have girlfriends or anything like that. Because we met so young, because our families have always been very supportive, we've always been comfortable with our sexuality. I know our parents were probably dis-appointed that we are gay, because it's easier for people to think of their children as heterosexual. But they loved us and accepted us. Our youth was never dumped upon us.

One of the great benefits of forming a stable, monogamous relationship at a very early age is that I'm still alive. Meeting Peter and falling in love and living together was just a path that I stumbled on. It could have been many other paths. Many friends and contemporaries from university days, like

Nigel, have died of AIDS, whereas I, quite by chance, missed the sexual free love revolution, which probably saved my life. Before meeting Peter I was intending to move to exciting Sydney, where I would have undoubtedly been caught up in the gay culture of the '70s with its alluring ethos of free love and very promiscuous sex.

It's wonderful that Peter and I have stayed together. It's hard for any two people, gay or straight, to form a relationship and stay together. But it's infinitely harder for homosexual couples, who aren't given the social recognition and encouragement accorded heterosexual couples. In fact, often families work to pull the relationship apart. Not in our case.

Back home from Europe we moved in with my parents, who have always loved Peter. In fact I think they love him better than they love me. They were very inclusive of him and, from the outset, he was fully accepted into my family and I was accepted into his. We finished our degrees — I have an MA in History, he has a degree in English — and went teaching. You might think teaching would be a dangerous profession for gays, because of unfounded parental homophobia, but actually most of your colleagues are liberals and sensitive — I call them humanists, in that they're more understanding than most people.

We lived in New Zealand for about three years, saving hard, then travelled through Argentina, Brazil and Chile, before flying to Europe, where we lived for another two years. We lived and taught in London, frequently toured the Continent and, once again, shared our lives, doing everything together.

At the end of the '70s we returned to New Zealand and decided we wanted to buy a farm. We moved back to my parents' house and spent a year teaching and saving hard.

In 1983 we bought 10 acres at Bethell's Beach for $46,000. We were lucky with the price, which was very cheap. In those days the Bethell's Road hadn't been sealed and the area was considered the back of beyond. As I was teaching in Otahuhu and Peter was teaching in Panmure, we spent the first year commuting right across Auckland every day. We spent a great deal of time, energy and whatever money we had doing the place up. Besides continuing with our teaching, we developed the farm and our poultry business. Three years later we moved to our new farm on 26 acres closer to town.

We've had to create our own path through life, staying together because we love each other. Our travels, saving for and developing the farm, and our political interests have kept us attuned to one another. Two strong-willed people, we surmounted difficulties and just went about our business. It's amazing how the time has flown. You blink, and 10 years have gone by. Blink again, and 20 have vanished.

We have never suffered overt discrimination for being gay, perhaps because we have always been very upfront. Also our political affiliations, our professional lives and the friends we've chosen have meant that, apart from a few well-known MPs, we've not met any openly homophobic people. If you're self-sufficient and confident, you don't invite discrimination. Most bigots are cowards and will only home in on the weak. If you don't see yourself as a victim, if you're strong, they'll leave you alone.

Which isn't to say that there aren't people out there who won't attack and bash gays, but I've never been unfortunate enough to encounter them. There may have been times when I haven't got a job because of being gay, but no one has ever given my sexuality as the reason. Certainly I've never suffered discrimination within the Labour Party for being gay, and this is one of the reasons I've supported the party so strongly over the years. It's a very humanistic party that delivers beyond the rhetoric. It's easy to say a party is gay supporting, but the Labour Party has proved its support: we've had a gay president, we have the only openly gay MP, and the party picked me for a seat they knew they'd win.

Despite never being overtly discriminated against, Peter and I were always very conscious that our sexuality was against the law. As gay men, we were not equal in this society. We frequently considered and debated questions of morality and the individual's place in society with friends and Labour Party colleagues. When an issue that strongly affected our own lives, namely the Gay Law Reform Bill of 1986, came up for discussion, it was natural we'd get involved.

I organised what was perhaps the largest meeting to take place in Auckland during the Gay Law Reform campaign. I was chairman of the Labour Party for the region at the time, and I set up a debate pitting Fran Wilde and Gary Taylor, a local city councillor, against Keith Hay and Barry Reid in the Massey High School hall. I chaired the meeting. Over 1100 people attended, and more were turned away. The Christian network bussed people in, and Auckland's lesbian community network bussed people in as well. We had at least 300 gay women and their supporters present, and an even larger number of fundamentalists. The Henderson police came, took one look and said, 'There'll be a riot.' Another 13 officers were sent for. But through circumstances, and my fairly forceful personality, order was maintained, the debate took place and excellent publicity ensued. I'm very proud of that meeting.

My involvement in this campaign boosted my political

interests and the next year, with Peter helping me all the way, I stood as the Labour candidate for Albany. It's a party tradition that aspiring MPs are encouraged to stand somewhere hopeless the first time around, to see if they can do it. In 1987 Albany, then held by National's Don McKinnon, was considered a hopeless Labour seat. I took three months' leave from school and worked very, very hard to be elected. I discovered I really enjoyed campaigning. It's hard work, but I took to politics with a lot of energy and enjoyment.

The 1987 campaign was a great demonstration of the excellence of Peter's and my relationship. It's a very successful partnership both in our public life and in private. We have a great deal in common. We're both interested in politics, we share the same philosophy of democratic socialism, we're keen on farming and gardening. We have very complementary personalities in that he's very practical and I'm much more ideological. Best of all, we're not competitive. Often, if people are too similar, there's friction in the relationship. You have to be complementary, but travelling the same road.

Our partnership is critical to my work. When I said I wanted to be an MP, Peter said, 'That's fine, I believe in you, I'll support you, it's something I want to happen.' Peter's not a public person — he doesn't like public speaking — but he's an excellent organiser and he's very good at inspiring and co-ordinating people. So I'm the public face of the campaign and Peter's the organiser. He runs my campaigns, he's on the New Zealand council of the Labour Party, he's the chairman of the Auckland region of the party. Both of us have a fair amount of energy and we're very much a political household.

It turned out that 1987 was a great year for Labour. Even

though I lost, I got 10,500 votes, which is more than I got when I won the Te Atatu seat. I have never fallen into the delusion that the voters think I'm wonderful. It's the Labour Party they're voting for, not me. Still, losing the election was quite hard, because you expend so much energy and time, and then suddenly it's all over. But I resolved that I wanted to be an MP, so I spent the next two years building a power base within the Labour Party.

Of course, these were very difficult years in the party, with the division between Roger Douglas and David Lange. I was very much with the left wing of the party, a natural ally of people like David Lange, and particularly Helen Clark, Ruth Dyson and Lianne Dalziell, people with whom I am philosophically very comfortable.

I got personally caught up in the great right-versus-left struggle for control of the Labour Party with the Te Atatu candidate selection of 1990. Michael Bassett, who had been quite a strong supporter of mine in the past, announced he would not stand again. Within the Labour Party it was widely assumed I was his logical successor because I'd taught at Te Atatu's Rutherford High and had been the candidate for Albany, which borders Te Atatu. However, Bassett, a very strong opponent of David Lange, Ruth Dyson and the so-called party machine, backed Dan McCaffrey, Richard Prebble's electorate secretary. I was held up as the champion of the left wing, and McCaffrey represented the right. The candidate selection in Te Atatu became a turning point in the Labour Party because it was the final rupture between the two wings of the party, and was probably the most disreputable and disgraceful drama to occur in the Labour Party in many years. The conflict ended with me losing the nomination to McCaffrey, who went on to lose the seat which had, until then, always been Labour. I spent the 1990 campaign helping friends like Judith Tizard with their Labour campaigns.

This stressful time made me resolve to fight the good fight and bring the Labour Party back to where it had been. I was determined to be the Te Atatu candidate in 1993 and, as soon as the 1990 election was over, I started working studiously in the electorate, setting up branches and enrolling everyone I knew in the party. When nomination time came around again in 1992, no one stood against me. McCaffrey had fled. I was reasonably confident that Labour would regain the electorate, which we did. Now, as a member of Parliament, I've discovered my time is totally absorbed by work, in which I really take a great deal of pride and pleasure.

Which brings us to my decision to come out. Why did I decide to be an openly gay MP? Three reasons, really.

Number one: I was comfortable and secure in my own sexuality, but I'd not arrived at that easily. As a teenager it was very difficult for me to come to accept my sexuality, perhaps because I never met anyone who said he was homosexual. I suspected that there were homosexuals out there somewhere — I wondered if certain television actors were gay — but no one ever actually admitted they were. I think it's very important for young gays and lesbians in New Zealand to see so-called authority figures, like teachers, doctors and politicians, come out proudly and say they are gay. So I came out for young gays and lesbians in our country. If that sounds a bit altruistic, my second reason for coming out — it's nice to be the first — isn't quite so idealistic. Along with the pride, there was a degree of vanity in being the first openly gay MP.

The third reason for coming out is that I believe my

sexuality to be a very positive part of my life. It's shaped my own personal political philosophy. As a teenager growing up in a Catholic environment I came up against the hypocrisy of a religion whose heroes preach love while actually practising the religion of oppression. I experienced the Christian Brothers' institutional brutality — the smacking, the strap and the verbal put-downs. It created an environment where boys like me, who were a bit sensitive, who didn't like sports, who didn't fit in, were made into outsiders, marginalised and unvalued.

I now realise that being an outsider can be positive. You don't accept the status quo, you start to look around and question the society in which you live. When I got to university I realised that there were other outsiders, too. Maori and Pacific Island people, women — there's a whole basket of outsiders in New Zealand, and I had an empathy with them. Poor people are outsiders in our society, too. My parents were poor. Being working-class New Zealanders, without much money, they lived in a much more restricted environment than the professional parents of my university contemporaries. Being an outsider made me realise society was hitting on me for being gay. I realised a lot of other people were being discriminated against too, and this recognition of social injustice drew me to social democracy. In another era — in the '30s, for example — I would probably have been a Communist. But by the '70s Communism had become, for me, a discredited philosophy. So I became a strong social democrat.

Being gay has been pivotal in my personal development and my life. So when I prepared to give my maiden speech in Parliament — the one time a new parliamentarian can talk, uninterrupted, about his or her life, influences and beliefs — I decided, this is it, I'm going to talk about being gay. All the other MPs had to sit there and listen. Mr Banks ostentatiously read a newspaper the entire time. Graeme Lee stared at me with a look of absolute horror on his face. Another politician, a closeted gay, fled the chamber. Of course I'm not the only gay MP. There are a number of others, but they're in the closet. This particular National MP departed, ashen-faced.

The next morning I was a bit naughty and I wrote him a note saying, 'I'm very sorry you had to leave the chamber and miss my speech. Here is a copy of it. I hope you will read it and learn something.' He never acknowledged it. He's a constant reminder to me of how tragic and self-oppressed life in the closet is. I feel empowered and confident every time I meet him. I feel very sorry for him as an individual, but I also feel a certain degree of contempt.

After this speech I expected a deluge of mad letters from crazed bigots and homophobes. But in fact there've been very few. The letters have run eight-to-one in favour. I've had many wonderful letters from young gays and lesbians, and some very old ones, who've seen snippets in the paper or heard me on the radio. Most live isolated lives in small towns in the Deep South, Otago and the Far North. Usually they sign their letters, but some keep anonymous. Either way, the message they write is: 'Chris, thank you for what you've done. You said what I wanted to say. You've stood up for us, and that's great.'

Richard
Huntington

When I was born in Napier, in 1966, my mother was 44 and my father 52 years old. I might have been a bit of an accident, but if I was, I'm sure my parents thought I was a pleasant one. We lived in Napier South, in a small house with an outside toilet. It had been my maternal grandparents' home, and my uncle and aunt lived next door. Dad grew up in the Depression, which made him careful with money. He was always telling me, 'Save what you've got. Don't be extravagant.' He was a draughtsman, and retired the year after I was born. Growing up with both parents at home all day meant we spent a lot of time together. Before I was five they decided to show me New Zealand and we travelled the country in our little Ford Prefect.

A serious child, I was always fascinated with electronics and science. I spent a lot of time reading science books and drawing diagrams of things I wanted to make. Mum used to tell the story about how, when I was three or four, I'd go around the house with her, putting all sorts of appliance plugs in her pockets. One day someone came to visit and I said, 'Look! Mummy's plugged in, but she's not switched on!'

I discovered radio broadcasting and became entranced

with the feeling of being in touch with the world through the radio. By the age of six I had decided to become an electronics engineer. Whenever we went out to the town dump — one of my favourite places — I'd look for old radios and electric stuff to fix up. When I was seven, a local radio announcer came to my school fair to do the announcing and play music. I was fascinated and he invited me to watch him do a children's programme in the studio. The studio was amazing: lots of lights, buttons and connections everywhere. I was in technology heaven, working out what everything did. At home I built my own studio, placing speakers inside and outside the house so I could play radio announcer.

My primary school teachers were really supportive. One arranged for me to make disco sound-to-light equipment for the school. I became the school technician, setting up the microphone and cueing the music at assemblies. Through a family friend I met the music teacher from intermediate school and repaired his record player. We became friends and, when I moved up to intermediate, he arranged for me to manage the school's electronic gear. I organised the sound and lights for school dances, and made speaker cabinets in metalwork and woodwork classes. He encouraged me to learn to play an instrument but I never had the patience. I found it immensely frustrating when I couldn't instantly play the music I wanted to play.

About this time I made my first best friend, Neil, and from then on always had at least one best friend. When his family moved to Auckland I visited them and loved the exciting big city. But I was happy in Napier, with lots of friends and fun things to do. I was popular. Everyone knew I would fix their broken TVs and stereos for free. I didn't bring friends home much, though, because I felt my parents never totally approved of them. When I brought someone home they'd often say, 'Oh, he's so immature!'

I felt close to my friends and, from about 10 years old, was aware of a strong attraction to other guys. This didn't bother me particularly, because I was friendly with both boys and girls, though the girls I liked were always tomboys. In form two I was strongly attracted to a couple of boys and wanted to be closer to them, physically and emotionally. Once, when I was visiting one of them, he sat down beside me on his bed. I had an overwhelming urge to put my arm around him and be close to him, which I did. His strong reaction — he yelled, 'What the fuck do you think you're doing?!' — shocked and scared me.

When a similar approach to my other friend got a similar reaction, my confidence was dashed and I realised I had to hide these feelings. From then on, although most of my friends were boys I felt attracted to, I never let them know that. I didn't stop being physically affectionate, though, and if two of us were working together at one desk, say, I'd put my arm around my friend. But I was careful that this touching never become an overt expression of my feelings of attraction.

I've always been keen to learn, and was thrilled to start Napier Boys' High School, eager to met new people and tackle new subjects. My music teacher transferred at the same time, and kept me at my technical initiatives. I studied English, maths, science and geography. But I really wanted to spend every waking minute studying electronics. I would spend most of the year concentrating on electronics until exam time, when I'd study like mad and pass my other subjects.

Napier Boys', already a sports-oriented school, was rugby mad. I enjoyed running and phys. ed. but I hated team sports and always have — right from primary school, where Mr Tasker would call the students who didn't like rugby 'sissies' and 'pansies'. I rebelled against being told which game I had to like. If the ball came my way, I ran in the opposite direction. At Napier Boys' I was excused from rugby because I was busy with my technical work, which was so highly respected I was one of the few non-rugby- playing students to be made a prefect.

In my third form year I had an interesting experience with a boy on whom I had an incredible crush. The fact he was unpopular and got picked on attracted me. I was sym-pathetic towards boys who didn't quite fit in, who weren't totally liked. Our class went camping up the Esk River, cycling 20 kilometres up the valley before pitching our tents. Someone put jam in his sleeping bag and damaged his tent. He ended up sleeping right beside me, outside the pup tent I was sharing with another friend. During the night it started to rain, so he rolled inside. I spent the night wide awake, feeling him pressed up against me. Being that near to someone I liked was an incredible experience.

The next year our French class went to New Caledonia — my one overseas trip so far. Our French teacher, an incredibly effeminate married man, was hassled endlessly. Kids would call him 'poof' to his face. When he caned them, they'd come back to class saying, 'He's such a poof! I didn't feel it,' even though I knew they were hurting. In New Caledonia they hassled him so much he had a nervous breakdown, which was pretty horrible. It left quite an impression on me.

During the fifth form my mother fell ill, with cancer, and died at the end of my sixth form. We'd always been close and I'm very glad that, during her last few months, we had the time to talk about life, and Mum became a really close friend as well as a mother. In the days immediately following her death I felt a strong mixture of sadness and relief — sadness because I'd lost my mother, but mostly relief because during her last few months she'd been in extreme pain and I'd felt great frustration at being unable to ease her suffering. That same year I lost a good schoolmate to cancer as well. Mum's death was very unexpected. When I was about 10 Dad had got sick, with angina, and was laid up for some time. Mum and I had discussed the possibility of his death and I was quite prepared for him to die first. Ironic that it happened the other way around.

All through high school I hoped something romantic might happen, but it never did. In the sixth form I fell in love for the first time, with Richard, a boarder. Although nothing physical ever happened, I know he liked me because we spent so much time together. I'd get up first thing on a Sunday morning and go and watch him play soccer. Whenever he could get out of the hostel he'd visit my house and play with my computers and talk. My memories of him are very intense. Tiny things, like his body scent, gave me an incredible high. This was a very special relationship, and I was really sad when seventh form finished and we went our separate ways.

Nowadays I'm astonished, and quite envious, when old schoolmates tell me about their sexual relationships with other boys at school. I had no idea anything was going on.

I didn't know any gay people, especially none my age. I thought that gays were older. There was one boy at school who claimed he was gay, but I never believed him. I thought he was just teasing me when he talked about his sexual exploits. He had me sussed, though, because he'd say, 'I know you'd like to do this stuff.'

At age 17 I shifted to Auckland to go to university, and moved into O'Rorke Hall, a university hostel, where I ended up living in a glassed-in verandah facing the Globe Hotel. I didn't take to hostel life. I was used to a very small family circle and couldn't handle being with hundreds of people. I hated eating in the dining hall, so I skipped most meals and lived on takeaways. I went from having lots of friends and a definite role to knowing no one and no one knowing me. Shy and homesick, I headed back to Napier whenever I could, and kept running the sound-and-light shows for the school socials.

I'd so looked forward to starting engineering studies but quickly lost interest when I found first-year engineering to be a repeat of sixth and seventh form. I started to skip lectures, and passed only three out of seven papers, which ruled out engineering as a professional option. I know Dad was quite concerned, but by this time I was so enthusiastic about Campus Radio that it didn't worry me.

Campus Radio was my one exciting discovery at university. After wandering past the studio a few times I plucked up the courage to introduce myself to the technician. He had a workshop filled with amazing electronic equipment — expensive stuff which had always been out of my reach financially. When I said I was interested in the technical side of radio he gave me a big list of quite yucky repair jobs. I attacked these with great enthusiasm and fixed everything in about a day. This made me instantly popular — so much so I was immediately hired, at $25 a week.

Second-year varsity I switched to a Bachelor of Science course, majoring in computer science, which I knew would be easy, and got all As that year. I left O'Rorke and went flatting with another Napier boy, David, and met his friends, some of whom I really fancied. We'd take fun weekend trips down to Lake Taupo, where his parents had a house. Big changes were happening at the radio station, too. We switched from AM to FM, and Campus Radio became BFm. That Christmas break I helped build the new studios, my first full-time paid job.

Apart from a couple of lecture buddies, I still hadn't made many friends, and didn't feel part of the social scene at the station. The radio crew tended to sit around smoking dope, which didn't appeal to me. I found them amusing, but kept to myself. My big discovery in my second year was the gay students' group. Reading their noticeboard I learned about the gay student dances held in the lower common room. Through BFm I had the keys to the upper common room, from where I could see down into the lower common room. Whenever the gay dances were on, I'd go into the top common room and sneak peeks downstairs, hoping to see someone like myself, someone I could relate to.

Around this time I read a *Listener* article about a gay show on Wellington's Access Radio, broadcast at 11 o'clock on Saturday mornings. I drove all over Auckland trying to pick up the station on my car radio, and found I got the best reception down by the Shore Road playing fields. Every Saturday morning I'd park in a little accessway in the middle of the playing fields, surrounded by football players, and listen to gay radio. The show was my first contact with the gay community.

In 1986, my third year at university, BFm combined with Auckland's Access Radio to broadcast throughout the holidays. Access had a gay radio show every Saturday morning and I always made sure I had an excuse to be at work so I could see the gay people go in and out. For the first time ever I saw a gay guy my own age. His name was Stephen and I found him very interesting and attractive. I always chatted to him, but there was no way I felt confident enough to talk about my sexuality or my feelings. I assumed Stephen thought I was merely being friendly. Later, after I'd come out, he told me he was quite aware of what was going on.

Around this time I encountered the 'Men against Sexism' discussion group recording a documentary on rape at BFm. They were an amazing group of guys who related to one another in a wonderful way, talking about their feelings and being physically affectionate with one other. All sorts of thoughts ran through my mind, like, 'Are they gay?' I was very attracted to one guy there, Shaun, who was about my height. (I was shorter than most guys I met and really noticed anyone my height.) I helped them with their recording, and when some editing worked really well they got excited and Shaun put his arms around me and hugged me. Nothing like this had ever happened before. I felt I'd found a group of kindred spirits and was determined to get to know them, but felt I was on the outside looking in.

The group met at Newman Hall on Thursdays at seven o'clock. The first time I went I was shaking, terrified about going in. I hesitated for about half an hour before finally working up the courage to knock on the door. The guy who opened it seemed surprised to see me. He went 'Oh!' and asked me to wait for a moment while he went and had a chat to the others. I stood there, feeling there was still a closed door between where I was and where I wanted to be. When he invited me in, I realised they were discussing really personal stuff, and it was awkward to introduce someone in the middle of the meeting.

'Come back next week,' they said, 'and be on time.' I was relieved, excited, but still unsure.

The next week I arrived to find everyone was sitting on cushions in this beautiful room, looking incredibly friendly. They were happy to have me there, which felt good. Quite by chance that night's discussion topic was homosexuality! I was shocked and didn't know how much I should say. I'd become quieter since my school days. Leaving home and my time in the hostel had made me very shy. People talked about their feelings for women as well as men. I listened intently but didn't say much. When someone asked me, 'So, Richard, have you ever had feelings for other men?' I replied, very noncommittally, 'I guess so. Sometimes.' Which felt like a huge admission to make.

My two years with the group were an incredible catalyst. I found something I'd been looking for — a group which felt like a real family — and I had incredibly strong affections for some of the guys. Two years after my first meeting — by now I was 22 and in my fifth year at university — we revisited the topic of homosexuality. By this time I was pretty clear about the fact that I was gay, and two things encouraged me to come out to the group. The first one was, a couple of weeks previously Shaun had come out and I identified with what he was saying. I saw him going places I wanted to be. I didn't want to be left behind. The second was the recent arrival of an openly gay man called Lee, who challenged the group's attitudes to sexuality. I talked with Lee privately and came out to him.

So, during our homosexuality discussion, I came out and said, 'I'm gay.' Everyone was supportive but surprised. I guess I'd kept my secret really well.

Later that week I was working late with Frankie, the lesbian production manager at BFm. I really loved Frankie and always talked with her about all the stuff I was going through. This particular night a gay dance was on directly opposite the station. I was watching people arriving and I had finally arrived at the stage where I wanted to go inside too.

Frankie came out and said, 'What's on?'

Without even thinking, I said, 'A gay dance. I've always wanted to go to those.'

'Let's go,' she said, and taking me by the hand she led me into the dance.

At first I was overwhelmed and just looked at the interesting people. There was the university custodian, a big butch guy I'd always been in awe of, dressed up in cowboy gear. I was amazed to discover he was gay.

Going to the dance inspired me to go to my first meeting of the gay students' group. Overcoming my usual nervousness, I walked into the middle of a planning meeting for the university's Gay Visibility Week. Accustomed to organising the technical side of these sorts of events, I got involved.

Visibility Week opened with a champagne breakfast. The gay students had invited a lot of well-known people like Richard Northey, the MP. I had a great time, and when a photographer from the *Auckland Star* organised a photo, I thought, 'Yeah! I'm into this!' That afternoon, one of the crew at the radio station said, 'Great photo of you in the *Star*!' There on the office noticeboard was a picture cut from page two, with me right in the front, under the big headline: 'Gay students celebrate Gay Pride Week.' I thought, 'Uh-oh! I'd better come out to a few people.'

I was apprehensive about how my flatmate, Andrew, would take the news. We'd been friends since high school and I'd always perceived him as anti-gay. I had to tell him, but kept putting it off. When I finally told him, I covered myself by saying, 'I know you're really homophobic, but . . .' His response was, 'I'm not! I'm not! It's okay that you're gay.' The funniest thing was, about five minutes after our talk, we sat down to watch TV and there's a film about a young gay guy coming out to his family. I had no idea it was going to be on. As we watched in silence I thought, 'Andrew probably thinks I planned this!' For a while, Andrew and I weren't quite sure how to relate to each other and things were a bit tense. But everything soon got back to normal.

After Pride Week and coming out to everyone in Auckland, I felt confident enough to go down to Napier and tell Dad. Easter was coming up and I decided to drive down, walk in the door and say, 'Hi Dad, I'm gay.' But when I arrived I couldn't do it.

Come the final morning, I knew I had to. Dad and I were sitting in the sunshine, making small-talk, and I just came out to him. I explained I hadn't told him earlier because I'd only just fully realised it myself. He was really good about it.

'We just thought you were a very quiet boy,' he said.

When we said goodbye, hugging on the verandah, I realised he was concerned that my new life might mean I'd leave him behind. I now feel much closer to him. I value our relationship a great deal more, and visit whenever I can.

Besides Unigays, I got involved with the Young Gays Group. Once again, I was really apprehensive about going in. The Young Gays guys were camp, quite bitchy, but friendly too. I found them fascinating. I made lots of new friends through Unigays and Young Gays, and started facing an issue that was totally new to me — really wanting a lover.

One night I tagged along with a couple of guys to Staircase, the gay nightclub in Fort Street. I'd never been to a nightclub or a bar before. When I saw a really cute boy looking at me, I thought, 'He doesn't look gay. He must be straight and he's only here for a look.' The other guys started dancing, and dragged me on to the dance floor with them. At school I'd been so busy working the technical things, I'd never danced. I loved it, and danced non-stop for two hours. I became a Staircase regular.

There was a long break between my coming out and my first sexual experience. One night at Staircase a reasonable-looking guy, who was quite drunk, asked to go home with me. I wasn't wildly attracted to him, but thought, 'If I don't say yes, maybe no one else will ever ask me!' We went back to my place and had sex, but I was quite disappointed in a way. Although it was really exciting, I regret having done it with someone I didn't really like.

That year Joe Kelleher facilitated a gay men's health conference at university, with lots of good workshops. By now I was a workshop junkie and was eager to go. However, I found it quite scary because I didn't identify with the other guys, who were all much older than me. One workshop ended with everyone standing in a circle holding hands. I was holding hands with a young guy, aged about 17, who I had assumed to be some gay dad's straight son. When he didn't let go of my hand I paid more attention to him, and realised he seemed intensely interested in me. His name was Danny, and we stayed together for the rest of the workshops.

I fell for Danny almost instantly. For the first time I was part of a couple, rather than part of the group. I was elated when he gave me his phone number and asked to see me again. I was on cloud nine because for the first time someone I was keen on seemed keen on me.

A couple of days later Danny and I got together in his flat. We sat down at opposite ends of the couch. I wanted to tell him how much I liked him, but couldn't think of the words. He looked at me, said, 'The feeling's mutual,' and moved over and put his arms around me. It was mind-blowing. He helped me relax by singing along to some music on the stereo and we lay down on the couch together. Looking back, I think he wanted to sleep with me right then, but I was so naive I didn't expect anything like that to happen! We didn't even kiss — just cuddled. I was completely infatuated. For a couple of weeks I saw him frequently, usually at the supermarket where he worked. I'd buy something I didn't need just so I could talk to him at the checkout.

Then our relationship, which had begun brilliantly, started to go wrong. When I realised that it wasn't working out between us, Danny suggested I see a counsellor he knew. What he didn't tell me was that he was actually in a relationship with this guy. Totally unaware of the situation, I saw this counsellor and confided my feelings for Danny and my hopes for the future. At first it seemed all very friendly. Then he suddenly confronted me with, 'Keep your hands off Danny! If you try to win him, you'll have a fight on your hands and you'll lose!' This was most upsetting, and when Danny said he wanted us to be friends, nothing more, my hopes and dreams were totally dashed. I was shattered.

At this time I was still at university part time but giving it very low priority, being more interested in becoming part of the gay community. Carl, a friend from the gay students' group, had been raving about this incredibly cute American boy, Charles Bracewell. I saw Charles at Staircase and he said, in his cute American accent, 'Care to dance to Kylie?' We became great friends, went flatting together in Grey Lynn, and I got involved in many of Charles's performance and music projects.

I was involved in ALGY, the Auckland Lesbian and Gay Youth group, and in 1989 and 1990 went to two terrific youth festivals. I became involved in Gayline, the telephone counselling service. I was learning about the gay community and wanted to do something positive for it. Creating a gay radio programme seemed to be a natural step, so in 1990 Charles and I launched BFm's Sunday night gay radio show, 'In The Pink'.

Despite being at BFm for several years, I'd still not done much announcing. I preferred to operate the equipment. With 'In The Pink', I saw Charles as the personality and me as the technician, which was how we started. Charles was the controversial host and I did the technical work. Gradually, though, I've become more of a co-host. Our four years on air have been really rewarding. It's great meeting guys just coming out who've been discovering the gay community through the show.

I haven't finished my degree, but this hasn't had a negative effect on my career. As a freelance technician, I rely more on my reputation, which is excellent, than any official qualifications. I still work at BFm, on contract, and free-lance elsewhere. I'm building a client base and picking up recording studio work. I enjoy working on music, and mixing, being creative and helping other people being creative.

Whenever I work someplace new, I don't mention my sexuality but leave clues that people will recognise, like my rainbow rings, because I like people to know I'm gay. I enjoy meeting other gay people and talking about gay things, so encourage others to come out to me.

It was a couple of years before I got over Danny. After giving myself so deeply that first time, I'm more careful when it comes to romance. I tend to fall for someone, in quite a big way, about once a year or so. The boyfriends I've had since Danny started out as friends, then became lovers, then changed to being very good friends. I really enjoy my ex-boyfriends — we're very close and talk about everything.

I'm happy. When I first came out, I was desperate to have a lover, but that mood has passed. Of course I would love to meet someone really sweet, but I've got many friends who give me a lot of love. My life continues to be an exciting and sometimes surprising series of discoveries about myself and the world. I guess I'm still learning what coming out really means.

Marc Bensemann

I was born in 1954 in Auckland, to two conventional parents. I have a younger sister and brother, and am of German and Scottish descent, a fifth-generation New Zealander. My pioneer forefathers arrived in Motueka, Nelson, in 1842, on the *St Pauli* from Hamburg. My family spoke German at home until World War Two.

My father, the youngest boy in a family of eight, left home aged 16 and did well in business. I grew up in a successful middle-class home. My family skied and sailed. Such upper-middle-class pursuits were important to my parents as signs of doing well.

We moved a lot when I was young. I went through six different primary schools. Consequently I've always felt something of an outsider. That feeling of being on the outside looking in is a wonderful qualification for a journalist.

When I was 13 my family moved to Christchurch and I entered Christchurch Boys' High School, a single-sex school, Christchurch's version of Auckland Boys' Grammar. I wasn't in the top class, but I wasn't in the bottom one either. To me, school was eight hours of awfulness every day. I wasn't happy. I never did any work and fluked my way through exams. When my younger brother joined the school and was put into a higher third form class than I had been in, I thought, 'Well, that's it. What's the point of trying?' Fortunately I was a book worm. So, even though I didn't swot, I got School C. It was the same with UE, which I had to sit. A teacher told me I'd never get it, but I did, with a reasonable pass mark.

Aged 13 or 14 I recall hearing about what men did in bed together and my first reaction was, 'That's impossible.' My second was, 'Why would they bother?' When I was 15 I heard about a beach near Christchurch where naked men went. I already had my driver's licence and the use of my mother's car, so I drove out there and walked up to this part of the beach. Sure enough, there were men with no clothes on, lurking. I lurked too, and peered over the top of the dunes. One guy saw me. He came over and lay down beside me. He had no togs on and suggested I took mine off as well. I did. We both had erections. 'Do you want me to touch that?' he asked. I didn't move. But when he did touch it, I leapt up and bolted in an absolute panic, dashing the three miles or so back to the car and the nearest habitation.

Two weeks later I was back. And for the next couple of years I'd go out there once a month or so, during summer. Quite a lot of sex play went on. I was very passive. I didn't suck guys, but they sucked me, or masturbated me. I didn't ejaculate, however. Excepting for wet dreams, I didn't ejaculate until I was 17. Then, sex got a lot better, although I was still pretty passive. I remember thinking of myself as quite spotty and gawky, and not at all attractive. I had always thought my brother was much better-looking than me. Around this time I was being jacked up on dates with the daughters of my parents' friends.

At home I was becoming completely impossible. After seventh form I started at university but hated it. I thought it worse than school. So I quit and got a job driving trucks. After nine months of this I was still being impossible at home, so my parents encouraged me to go to Australia.

I arrived in Sydney aged 19, dressed in a striped tanktop over a yellow shirt, houndstooth crimplene flares and platform shoes. I moved into the Pitt Street YMCA. The bathroom consisted of a row of showers with no doors or curtains, opposite a row of toilets, all of which had holes cut into the doors facing the showers. It was here, within a couple of days, that I got fucked for the first time. Now I asked for it, but I absolutely hated it. I didn't enjoy it.

I did various jobs. I drove a truck. I did welding for a while. I hitched across the Northern Territory and slept rough. Travelling through Adelaide I met a girl, Diane, and I had my first experience with heterosexual sex. It was wonderful, absolutely marvellous. 'I'm not a homosexual,' I thought, though I had never really thought I was anyway. I really enjoyed having sex with Diane. We went for records, like 12 times within 24 hours, that sort of thing. We were travelling around with another straight couple and we'd all make love in the same bed, but not touching the other couple. Actually, I can recall wanting to make love to him, not her.

During a phone call home, my parents said it was time I did something with my life. It had been two years since I'd left school and it was about time I studied for something. 'You've always liked writing,' said my father. 'Why not try journalism?'

So I came home and went to the journalism course at Wellington Polytechnic, a one-year course that was more prestigious in the profession then than it is now. This was 1975. I was 21 years old, taking classes with lots of 17- and 18-year-old school leavers. I had the advantage of age and experience. I wore denim suits, love beads, silver bangles and an earring. I had hitched around Australia. I wasn't exactly a Big Man On Campus, but for the first time I felt empowered and at ease. And so I found it easy to talk about myself as being bisexual. That was also helped by the fact that I lived with my girlfriend, Jill.

After graduation I got a job with the Christchurch *Press*, a bastion of conservatism. For the next three or four years I lived the heterosexual life. My girlfriend, Vicki, was a Catholic whose brother was a priest. I cared for her very much. We mixed with a big heterosexual group who went off on water-skiing parties, stayed at baches, that sort of thing. But at the same time I was also having sex with men on the beach and by now I enjoyed fucking and getting fucked.

I met Ian at the beach and fell in love for the first time. And, as soon as I fell in love, I knew I wasn't bisexual, I was gay. I was so in love with Ian (who, incidentally, is now dying in Sydney), I left Vicki for him. We got a puppy and set up house together in an old villa. When I came out, all my straight friends from my life with Vicki weren't sure about me. Their parents didn't know whether they should leave their kids alone with me.

Ian introduced me to drugs — marijuana, acid, speed. I grew dope, all those sorts of things, but never let it interfere with my job at the paper. Occasionally I'd go to work speeding but I kept my shit together, even though I wasn't working very well or conscientiously. I shot up heroin three times. Heroin was wonderful. A hooker named Jade cooked it up for us. But I was well aware of the dangers, so didn't get too involved with it. So there I was, leading this very conventional middle-class life, going to work every day and being a good journalist, or maybe not such a good one, and at night drugging myself up to the eyeballs.

Less than a year later Ian announced he was leaving me, to go and live with one of our friends. I had been dumped. I was totally desolate. I spent a year getting over Ian, then met Peter, a medical student.

Peter was a very cerebral type who found it difficult to be affectionate. When we met I was smoking dope heavily — dulling the ache of being left by Ian, I guess — and I'd smoke every day. I'd come home from work and automatically light up. When I look back now, I realise my emotional development had stopped. Peter and I had a strange, remote relationship. I don't want you to get this wrong. I loved him very much. I remember telling my best friend, Andrea, 'I'll never leave Peter.' (I've always tended to have two strong relationships running in my life at the same time: a 'best friend', who's often been a woman, and a lover.) Peter was very well hung, our sex life was great, but he never told me that he loved me.

In 1983, when I was 29, Peter and I decided to holiday in Europe. I arranged for friends to look after the house and the dog, and away we went for six months, touring the States, Italy, Greece, Turkey, Holland and Britain. It was absolutely marvellous. I came home, turned 30, met an American guy, Kurt, and fell madly in love. Peter and I broke up. He said, 'Stop seeing this guy, or I'll move out.' I told him he could move out.

Kurt was a swimming coach, with a fantastic body. At first he went back home to the States and the phone bills were phenomenal. Then he came back to live with me and it was really wonderful.

Kurt was a highly motivated person. He didn't like dope,

and very soon I stopped smoking it. It had become a real habit — psychological if not physical. Not having dope to lean on, and trying to get over my break-up with Peter, left me very depressed. So I went to a therapist and did psychodrama, working though all those feelings and healing myself. Let's face it, for five or six years my emotional life had been on hold, and then I'd gone through a divorce with Peter.

In 1988 Kurt was offered a great job in Auckland, at a pool run by two lesbians. He got the job partly because he was a gay man. So we moved up here and bought a house in the bush. I got a job at the *New Zealand Herald*. A few months after we arrived, Kurt started to get oral thrush, and we knew what that meant. So we both went and had the test, and were both HIV+. Kurt and I had been monogamous. His previous lover was HIV+. Mine wasn't.

So there we were. It was just Kurt and me. We had no support, no friends in Auckland, and felt very isolated. Kurt's family were all in America. For three years Kurt got sicker and sicker — it was a horrible period. As he got weaker I reduced my working hours to nurse him. Eventually I was working only three nights a week. Towards the end I told my bosses that a friend was dying and I needed time off to care for him. Wilson and Horton are very good employers, and gave me leave without pay.

Kurt and I didn't discuss in any depth what was happening to him. I did a lot of gardening; he just lay in bed and faded away.

Kurt died. He died in bed, at home, where I still live. He wasn't in our big bed, but a bed the hospital lent us. Kurt died while I was washing him. Caring for him was the best and worst experience of my life. Looking after Kurt was a wonderful thing. I've never done anything quite so real.

We had planned to have our ashes mingled and scattered in a lovely spot we'd found near Christchurch, but near the end Kurt decided he wanted his body returned home to America. So I had two funerals to get through. One here and one in the States.

The next year was terrible. I came back from the States and went back to work. I've always been quite efficient and I coped, but things were so bad I'm surprised I didn't die of self-neglect. I was crying every day, but I don't remember crying for myself. It was all for him. No one saw me grieve. I just locked all the feelings inside.

Looking for help, I joined a 12-on-12 peer support group and the Burnett Clinic's Wellness programme. I saw a therapist regularly, and, basically, I'm a new man after all that.

The guy who started 12-on-12 — he's dead now — also had the idea of starting Body Positive, an HIV+ self-help group. There was a desperate need for it, and it's been a howling success, even though we're still rocky financially.

There's such a feeling of isolation when you're HIV+. It's hard to explain, but gays will understand when I say it's just like coming out as a gay person. When you come out of the gay closet, you leave your previous life behind. Your family might still love you, but they don't know what it's like to be gay. You're different from everyone you knew. Coming out of the HIV+ closet is like coming out all over again. It's another journey of self-acceptance, another passage to finding new healing and well-being. Like gayness, it's a social stigma, but just as it's entirely possible to be content with your gay status, it's equally possible to be content with your HIV status.

People don't understand HIV. Working with gay people recently on an HIV affirming project — I now spend a large part of my life as an HIV activist — I wanted to put in a quote: 'If you're gay and you have reached a position of self-acceptance, would you want to be straight? If you're HIV+ and reach the same level of self-acceptance, would you want to be HIV-?' The others in the group who were HIV- couldn't understand it, and wouldn't use it.

HIV is the best thing that has happened to me. It's helped me define who I am and where I'm going. It's been a valuable tool, one that I never would have found otherwise, for focusing my life. An HIV diagnosis doesn't do this for everyone. Many die in miserable conditions, alone and rejected.

Having HIV is like really knowing you're going to die. Now I know everyone knows they're going to die, sort of, but do we really believe it? Can we accept it? With an HIV+ diagnosis, you know the odds are that you will die about 10 years after infection. You are forced to accept the foreknowledge of death.

An HIV diagnosis is different in other ways too. When you're diagnosed with cancer, you've got cancer. When you're diagnosed with leukaemia, you've got leukaemia. When you're diagnosed with a brain tumour, you've got a brain tumour. But when you're diagnosed with HIV, you haven't got AIDS, only the potential to get AIDS. You're not actually any different. You're not actually ill. I'm not sick now. Of course a lot of people do get ill. I've lost enough friends not to be under any illusions about that. But I don't believe that every HIV+ person will die within 10 years of infection. Some of us are going to live with it. You've got to have hope.

Some of the most motivated, strong, coping and caring persons I know are people with HIV. Being gay makes some people worse. Being HIV+ doesn't. Taking that double journey into prejudice changes people for the better.

Postscript: Marc is well and happy and living with the man he loves.

Mika

I was born on 8 February 1962, the Year of the Tiger, and I'm an Aquarian. I was adopted into a family where I was the second of three children, with an older sister and a younger brother.

I was never interested in searching for my birth parents, though I always knew I was Maori. This isn't as strange as it sounds — I mean, I could've been Rarotongan. Over the years I've learned my birth father, a Maori from the Ngapuhi people, was a wonderful singer and my birth mother, a Pakeha, was extremely beautiful. Apparently I have a biological sister, but we've never met. On my Ngapuhi side I count Te Rauparaha as one of my tupuna.

I am also of Kai Tahu and Kati Mamoe descent. My mother, that is, the woman who adopted me, was Maori, from the Kati Mamoe. She comes from an interesting family which includes that old couple, Fred and Myrtle Flutey, who have that famous paua-shell house at Bluff. On my Pakeha side I trace my family back to Lord Anderson, who signed Mary Queen of Scots' death warrant.

I grew up in Timaru which, to me, is the closest thing to the town in *Twin Peaks*, in that it looks utterly conventional but contains pockets of the bizarre. As a teenager I had a great bunch of lesbian friends who worked in the town's massage parlour. I was very close to a most marvellous woman — utterly divine and utterly rich (the two so often go together!) who would use nothing but the most expensive French crystal glasses.

Timaru is a very tough town, and many of the guys I went through school with are now in prison. Whenever I go south I visit Timaru and see all the people I grew up with, most of whom still live there. The old friends I can't deal with are these three really handsome guys I used to have sex with, right throughout school. They're married now and so fucked up in the head. They're introverted loners, leading the most dreadful lives. I know I should try to help them deal with their sexuality, but there are some people whom you just can't reach, and I'm too selfish to bother.

I've always been queer. Always. I can remember my first sex experience when I was aged around four. Another boy, called Anthony, and I were caught playing with each other, and I got the only hiding I ever had from Dad. I was so upset and frightened I climbed into the clothes basket and pulled all the clothes over on top of me. I knew about drag queens, too, from an early age. Carmen was the first drag queen I ever heard about. I remember, aged eight or nine, reading in *Truth* about these Maori boys in Wellington who dressed up as women, did stripteases and had wild parties. I thought, 'That's where I want to be!'

I came out at intermediate school. I recall being in a tent at a school camp with nine other boys and all of us jacking off. It wasn't truly gay sex, just adolescent experimenting — innocent and exciting.

Perhaps because I was such a big, strong kid who played rugby and was the fastest track athlete in the school, I didn't have much trouble dealing with high school homophobia.

At the age of 13, as a new kid at Timaru Boys' High, I gave the school assembly a lecture on Homosexual Law Reform. On mufti day I turned up at school dressed all in pink. The closeted gay kids didn't want to know me. The straight boys wanted to kiss me.

At high school there were three kids who were really out to get me. I took the first one on in a fight, and did him over badly. There was blood on the walls. I bailed the second one up in the school toilets. Inspired by *The Naked Civil Servant*, which I had just seen on television, I copied the famous scene where Quentin Crisp confronts a gay basher by saying, 'Why don't you sod off back to Brixton before everyone realises you're queer?' I said to this guy, 'I know you want me.' That frightened him off. And the last one I approached in front of around 200 kids and said, 'C'mon, let's fight. Do something now!' He backed off too.

My dad died of a heart attack in 1977, when I was 15. He was diabetic. Mum died 10 years later of a broken heart. The doctors came up with all sorts of reasons for her death — cancer, emphysema — but I know she died for love. She was a wonderful woman, the favourite of so many people. She was never a stage mother. And, if she had been, I probably would have rebelled against the theatre. The only thing Mum tried to keep me away from was tikanga Maori. She didn't want me to know anything about Maori culture. This, of course, made me determined to learn about it, and I secretly studied carving.

Mum came to terms with my sexuality when I was 16. When I came out to her, she bawled her eyes out at first, then sent me to a doctor. This was a time when I really needed to hear the truth about what it meant to be gay — and what did I get? A doctor who, when I told him I was sexually attracted to other males, replied that he knew of two other cases like mine. 'One committed suicide. The other's in Sunnyside Mental Asylum.' I can remember the conversation to this day. The doctor asked me, 'Do you think of little boys?' I said, 'Doc, I'm only 16.'

I was referred on to a psychiatrist who was, I later found out, a rigidly fundamentalist Christian. Mum came along for the first meeting and he acted very nice while she was in the room. 'I think I can fix your son,' he said.

At the next meeting, when we were alone, he turned nasty. 'Fruitcakes like you get done over, you know.'

We were brought up to trust doctors, so when he asked for a list of all my sexual partners, I gave it to him unquestioningly. Some of the guys on the list weren't even sexual partners — if I'd just kissed someone, his name went on my list. This bastard broke medical confidentiality by giving the list to my mother and my doctor!

The lasting effect of this event has been my distrust of the medical profession, though I can't say I had previously held people in authority in high regard. In fact I've always been rebellious, and my lack of respect for the 'proper channels' continued after I left school.

Mum confronted me with the list, and at first I was dumbstruck. She said, 'Look at all these people you've been with!' Luckily I was a very together 16-year-old. I couldn't see what was wrong with my sexual behaviour. In fact, even now I find it hard to understand why people get so hysterical over being gay. I think this inborn acceptance of who and what I am has been one of the real blessings of my life. I was furious about this doctor's action but I kept calm, sat down with Mum and told her, basically, to get over it, though I didn't use quite those words. I reminded her of all the good things about me — I was very athletic and had lots of friends. Once we'd talked, she was cool about it all, and was fine with it from then on. We didn't have a touchy feely relationship and never really discussed my sexuality again, but she always treated the friends I brought home with respect. The one thing Mum asked of me was not to mention it to my grandmother, and I respected her request. The rest of the family knew about me, though. Once, when all my aunties and cousins were visiting, we were looking at some photos of a party I'd been to. My cousin said, 'How come there are only boys in these photos? Where are the girls?' I replied, 'C'mon, all of you know I'm gay. It's no big deal. Get over it.'

After passing UE I quit school and went straight into hairdressing. Hairdressing was my job, but dancing was my life. From being a kid, dancing around the living room copying the *Happen Inn* dancers, to winning the South Island Disco Championship in 1980, I'd always loved dancing. I was born a great dancer. It's an innate talent in most Maori and Polynesian people. From school discos onwards, people have always been impressed with the way I could move. I was always a very keen singer too, and only gave it up at high school, which didn't teach singing.

In 1983 I won New Zealand's Flashdance Championship. The day after, I walked into the hair salon; said, 'I quit!' and proceeded to open up my own dance studio. I had no technical dance knowledge, but people only wanted to learn two types of dance — disco and break-dancing — so I taught them! If you've got confidence in yourself, people will follow you.

I've always enjoyed taking a challenge, becoming the best, then moving on. In 1984, even as I moved to Wellington to be an instructor at the New Zealand School of Dance, I was changing my focus more towards the theatre. I became a member of Te Ohu Whakaari, the Maori Theatre Company, from 1984 to 1988. In 1986 we performed at the Sydney Opera House during the Sydney Gay and Lesbian Mardi Gras. I was keen to promote Te Ohu Whakaari as a company of gay Maori performers and to make us a part of the Mardi Gras Arts Festival. But I was told to be quiet. I vowed that this would be the last time I would let anyone make me hide being gay. I've been totally open ever since.

I did my first solo show at Wellington's Depot Theatre in 1988, as part of the International Festival of the Performing Arts. I was keen to combine my singing, dancing and acting into one performance, which is why I love cabaret work so much. It's a chance to explore every talent I have, plus it puts me in direct communication with the audience. I feel most alive when I'm on stage — just me, the microphone and the audience. It's not important whether they're laughing, crying or simply listening. What's important is the connection between me and the audience. It gives the biggest buzz of all.

Also in 1988 I was cast in a television series, *Shark in the Park*, playing a very butch young policeman. I also played Carmen in her television biography directed by Geoff Steven. But television's my least favourite medium. First of all, television tends to stereotype performers, chew them up, then spit them out. Secondly, any television work is extremely limited in permitted content and time. Thirdly, it's run by gay executives and directors who reinforce the culture of the closet by never putting openly gay actors on screen. Gay roles are always given to supposedly straight actors. It's a double standard. They'd never give Maori or

Polynesian roles to dark-skinned Pakehas! Being Maori, being gay, being a drag queen or warrior: all these have worked for me rather than against me, which puts paid to all those lies about gay actors destroying their careers by coming out.

Since I started working in cabaret, film and theatre, my career has flourished and given me a great deal of personal satisfaction. I've performed cabaret at arts festivals in York, Edinburgh, Adelaide, the Barcelona Olympic España Arts Festival, and at the United Nations in New York. I've toured New Zealand for the Arts Council and performed at every Hero party.

Over the past three years or so, I've been embraced by a straight audience. Straight culture is now ready and eager to see an eclectic, cross-gender cabaret show because, through films like *Priscilla* and *Wong Foo*, it's realised how entertaining, challenging and exciting gay cabaret can be. There's a new audience out there who want more from an evening's entertainment than some Kentucky Fried Chicken and a couple of videos. If you can entertain them, they'll accept you. As the old cliché goes: after years of hard work I'm an overnight success!

Just as straight venues have changed, by welcoming gay and lesbian entertainers, I've noticed changes in gay and lesbian society. I find the misogyny I knew in early gay culture — a misogyny that created the men-only/women-only spaces that were so important in the '70s and '80s — isn't present in the new generation of gays and lesbians. They don't need those spaces to define themselves, as earlier generations did. The rigid stereotyping and prejudices of the earlier years have gone. I'm a great believer that you should never limit yourself through prejudice. I've never slept with a woman, but this isn't to say that I won't. I believe one should never say 'never'. I mean, I've never done drugs, but one day I might. Just as one day I might sleep with a woman. I might do a lot of things I've never done.

I'm always open to change, and my act is much more androgynous than when I started out. Although the straight media, insisting that any gay person who puts on a dress is a drag queen, call me a drag star, I no longer think of myself as one. For me, drag is a highly disciplined art form in which an artist works with the costume and the voice in creating this real woman. Mika doesn't pretend to be a real woman. I don't wear a dress. I don't have breasts, I have a penis. Sometimes I have Rastafarian hair and tattoos. So I cross and confuse the male/female boundaries.

Like the Topp Twins I've discovered that, although being gay is an important part of my persona, it shouldn't dominate the whole act. In fact, I rarely perform in gay clubs these days. This is a financial decision: gay clubs simply don't have the money. I've discovered that straight, white money is beautiful! Money doesn't have a preference. Money doesn't care if you're black, white or brown, gay or straight. I treat my career very much as a business, and have a press agent, a manager, an assistant and a PA to maximise every opportunity. I'm putting energy and money into the infrastructure of my business — maintaining a wardrobe of costumes, props, press releases, tapes, all those sorts of things.

I know that this constant focus on my career looks like egotistical self-promotion and that it irritates a lot of people. But if you don't do this sort of thing, you don't get work. This is how professional artists maintain their image, their visibility and their viability. Otherwise you're forgotten.

The busier I've become with my career, the more I tend to be a loner in my private life. I don't socialise as much as I used to. I do so much socialising for my job that I can't be bothered being polite in my own time. Often I just drive around for hours, looking at people, looking at what's going on, getting ideas for performance.

When I go out now to perform, I always enter and leave the venues with an assistant and a manager, who walk me in and out so I don't have to talk to anyone. It's a distancing thing, maintaining the mystique — something I learned in America. Don't hang around, otherwise you spoil the illusion. Onstage they see you as this tall, glossy, brown and beautiful person. But once you're offstage and those heels go off, you're back to being short and dopey. So you do the last number, shriek out, 'We love you all!', and while they're calling for more you're out the door, down the stairs, into the van and off.

It's a protection thing too. I've had two men stalk me — they've been dealt with now — but once you've achieved a certain level of notoriety you can get into rather ambiguous situations by being too friendly and available.

At the same time as my career has flourished, my private life has suffered, in that AIDS has taken a great personal toll. I've now lost 35 friends and co-workers and people close to me. I can look at a video of my Hero 3 show and say, 'He's gone. She's gone. He's gone.' I lost seven friends from that one show alone.

I've been a strong supporter of safe sex ever since the mid '80s, when we first learned that safe sex stops the spread of HIV. Safe sex needs to be taught everywhere and I find talking one-on-one a much better way to teach the safe-sex message than handing out leaflets.

As part of a Smoke Free health promotion a couple of years back, I took my cabaret act to 95 high schools around New Zealand. Everywhere I went kids would ask, 'Are you the man who sings "I Have Loved Me a Man"?' This invariably led to a discussion about gay issues and I find that kids, so long as you talk to them honestly and answer their questions directly, are very receptive to safe-sex and gay pride messages. One time at Tamaki College this kid called out, 'Are you all gay?' So I asked every gay person in my troupe to step forward. The three of us did, and all the kids yelled and cheered.

Here I am, from a little country in a distant corner in the world, and I've fucked with condoms since 1986. Yet in 1992, in Barcelona, in the heart of Europe, when two incredibly handsome Spanish boys took me to a disco, I discovered that no one there practised safe sex. This Spanish crowd danced until everyone was totally overheated and hysterical. Then these huge foam machines sprayed everyone with cool, foamy water, making our clothes almost non-existent. We were drenched, slippery and writhing together. The Spaniards all started having sex, no one caring about their partner's gender. No one cared about using condoms, either. It was as if they'd never heard of AIDS. I couldn't believe it.

Practising safe sex hasn't limited my sex life. My work means I'm constantly surrounded by beautiful young men — dancers and actors — some of whom I find very attractive. Whilst I've had a lover, Mohi, for four years now, we don't own each other. I have other lovers and so does he, and I encourage that. We love each other — I am more in love than when we first met — because we allow each other the space to grow and develop. Mohi and I have recently taken to arranging it so we have entire days together, just the two of us. We really treasure each other's company.

People find my sexual honesty hard to deal with. I'll meet someone, we'll have lunch, always, and I'll say, 'I'm going to seduce you soon and you're going to be my lover. Are you happy with that?' I have several lovers who are bisexual, something I never would have considered a few years ago. They have me, and they have their girlfriends too.

Falling in love with someone doesn't give you ownership over them. I'm not into controlling other people, either in my private life or my public one.

Even though I understand it, I don't subscribe to competition between performers, something which is very big in the entertainment/acting business. When I create my shows, I try to give space for every actor, dancer and musician to have their moment to shine.

Speaking spiritually, the very best thing you can do is remove yourself from the need to be better than anyone else. That way you become a better person. In the end, when I die, I die. I have to take my chances now and do my work as best I can. Some of my creations, like my role in *The Piano*, will live on after I'm gone.

Of all the cabaret shows I've done, I'm proudest of *Carmen's International Coffee Lounge*, which I co-created with John Draper and performed as part of the Hero 3 Arts Festival. Telling Carmen's story wasn't easy. It's taken years to get through the layers that she hides beneath. Carmen tries not to show the struggle and the heartache. All you hear is the 'fabulous' side — 'Everything was *fabulous*, darling!' Carmen edits out the nastiness, the cruelty and the hard times. I don't. I think everything should be told — the good and the bad. I refuse to brush anything aside. I answer any questions reporters ask me. The only questions I despise are, 'How gay are you? How Maori are you?' I confront the people who ask these sorts of questions. I don't give a fuck which paper or magazine they're from: I don't have to validate my life or my heritage for anyone.

Michael Hay

I was born 28 September 1952 in Auckland, at Cornwall Park Hospital. My mother went into labour six weeks early — she'd had pregnancy diabetes. When I was born I had mucus burn, and thrush in my mouth and throughout my system. I couldn't keep fluids down. I spent the first six weeks of my life in hospital, hooked up to tubes going in all directions. Mum used to visit me every day and, because she wasn't allowed to pick me up, she would pass the time by talking to me. This is why, I think, I have trouble hugging and touching people, and am so verbally tuned in to the world. For the first eight or nine months, Mum had great difficulty getting me to take any food at all.

I am the eldest of three boys. My father was in the New Zealand Navy. My mother was a school teacher. I was very close to my grandmother — in fact she was the first family member I came out to. My grandmother was born out of her time — she would have fitted in perfectly with today's society. She was an educated, sophisticated, wonderful woman of the world.

We lived in New Plymouth until I was 14, when we moved to Henderson. To continue my music studies — I'd studied the piano since early childhood — I went out-of-zone, to Avondale High School, the nearest high school that taught music as a School C subject. I'm gifted musically. Besides learning the piano I taught myself the violin and led the school orchestra. I have a good ear, not only for music but also for languages. I speak German, Spanish, French and Indonesian, and I recently learned Maori.

Being an out-of-zone pupil, living in a new area, I found it difficult to make friends. My feeling of isolation was accentuated by the fact that I knew I was different. I'd known I was different at intermediate school, but it didn't matter too much there. But at high school there was much more pressure to conform, to fix yourself up and fit in.

Sexually I'd been very active with other boys from a young age. But at high school I discovered not only that was I unable to identify the gay boys but that my approaches to other boys were publicised. Sometimes, however, I would get referred on. When someone rejected me he'd say, 'But why don't you try so and so . . .'

I had additional pressures put on me when Mum got very sick, which meant I had to run the household and care for my two younger brothers, aged around seven and nine, as well as doing my school work. As a result I had no time to make close friends. I have this picture of myself at this time as socially isolated and unskilled at trying to extricate myself from my loneliness.

In 1970 I went automatically, unquestioningly, to university which, instead of being liberating, terrified me. I still didn't know how to make contact with anyone. I recall parking my car up near the Wynyard Tavern and walking down to class past all the other students, feeling they were laughing and talking about me.

1970 was also the year I came out to myself. For the first time, aged 18, I put a label on what I was. Gay. Towards the end of this year I became very depressed. I longed for a friend, an older person, to help me cope with my life but ended up trying, unsuccessfully, to deal with it alone. I needed to talk to someone so I went to my GP, a Catholic. He was the first person I told I might be gay. He hurriedly brushed me off with a referral to a psychiatrist.

I couldn't bear the wait for the appointment and took an overdose of my mother's pills. When Mum came home we played a game of cribbage before I told her what I'd done. She called Dad at work. He came home and they took me to the hospital where I had my stomach pumped. The hospital doctor told me to go back home and concentrate on my exams. Although they cared very much for me, my parents weren't sure how to cope with this symptom of my distress.

When I eventually got to see a psychiatrist, I told him everything but the truth. I told him I was lonely and isolated but couldn't face telling him I was gay. I hoped he'd realise what was wrong. Instead he prescribed some anti-depressants.

In my second year at university I got into a disastrous relationship with a woman. We had no secrets from one another. I told her that I might fancy men but she should not take this personally. She waited until the night of the big medieval supper at the Goethe Club to tell me, in the car going home after this incredibly rich meal, that she was breaking up with me. Then she threw up all over the car. So ended 1971.

The next year I saw the noticeboard of the university's Gay Liberation Society. They were having a social evening. 'New people made welcome,' said the sign. I went along, sat down, and not one person spoke to me all night. I left without having met any gay people and never went back. I was totally lacking social skills. I believed myself to be ugly, spotty, unattractive. These wounds are with me still.

I got a summer holiday job working in the kitchens at Air New Zealand, an all-male environment. There was one guy there I really fancied. One night, when we were driving out to service a plane, I was sitting next to him in the cab of the truck with my legs up on the dash. He brushed his hand up against my thigh. I was excited but not sure what to do. Back at the kitchens I watched him slope off around the back. I didn't know what to do, so carried on washing dishes. Everyone finished for the day until it was just me and the supervisor, who kept sending huge trays of crockery through the machine for me to deal with. Eventually I made it out the back and there he was, still waiting for me. We both had raging hard-ons bulging through our white overalls. He drove me to the end of a deserted country road near the airport and we had sex in the back of his car. He was married. There was no future to the relationship. In fact there was no relationship.

In 1973, my last year at university — I was 21 years old, studying for my Masters in Political Science — I fell in love for the first time. I mean, total infatuation. I had noticed this guy on the periphery of our group of senior students who seemed lonely, isolated and unhappy. I started inviting him to the student cafe for coffee, and we'd talk about work and life. We began to exchange confidences. I told him I was gay. I knew he was straight and I didn't even fancy him at this stage, so I had no ulterior motive. But one day I woke up and everything was different. Suddenly I found myself completely besotted with him. I manoeuvred to go flatting with him, which only made the situation worse. Many nights I would end up in tears of frustration and unrequited love.

The following year I began my teacher training at Epsom Teachers College. There was one obviously gay person in the class, a flamboyant, very effeminate person. I couldn't stand him, but at a party one night I let him pick me up. We had sex and it was awful. I said, 'Don't be surprised if I don't acknowledge you tomorrow.'

I moved into a little one-person flat in Royal Oak. My personal life was confused. I hadn't integrated my gayness into my total personality. I had gay neighbours, but didn't socialise with them. Occasionally I'd have sex with a Samoan neighbour. I began a very difficult relationship with a hitchhiker I'd picked up. We'd have the most terrible screaming fights. This lasted two years.

I was an intellectual queer. Although I intellectually accepted the fact that I was gay, I had never talked about my feelings nor acknowledged them. I was comfortable around straights but awkward amongst gays. I'd present my gayness to straight friends as something a bit exotic, a bit exciting. I'd make jokes about it. Even now, I don't mix socially with gays, and this separation of the head and the heart persists.

Physically, sex is not a problem for me. Over the years I've gone to bed with lots of men. But letting them get emotionally close is a problem. 'If you want to get to know me,' I tell prospective lovers, 'you have to be patient. You need to pay close attention and keep a look out for the times when I'm feeling threatened. You need to see through the glib, articulate exterior to find the "real" me.' No easy task. I know I come across as an attractive, forthright, outgoing personality but, to me, it's a role I'm playing. I don't see myself as attractive at all.

Teaching wasn't for me. I felt the kids laughed at me. I

knew I'd commit suicide if I stayed in teaching, so quit and went to San Francisco, where I had friends, a straight couple who had invited me to visit any time.

I worked in their shop, a touristy place in Union Street, and picked up the first obviously gay customer who came in, even though he was short, spotty and ugly. I turned the charm on; he asked me out. He took me to a bar with a dance floor. I couldn't believe my eyes. All these really handsome men! My new friend encouraged me to chat to everyone. I went back to that bar every night. My New Zealand accent was a great social asset and I met lots of men.

I moved on to London and worked in a Soho market research office for the next seven years. I flatted with an assortment of very straight New Zealanders and Australians, and kept my 'real' life and my 'gay' life separate. Apart from a couple of unhappy, unrequited gay romances, nothing was happening in my life, so I came home.

Back in New Zealand, I felt back at square one, desperately lonely and depressed. So I made a plan of action to learn how to get comfortable in gay venues. Every night, after work, I would go to the Alexandra Hotel, then Auckland's gay hotel, for a couple of hours to read the paper and have a couple of drinks. I had to go on week nights, because on weekends it was filled with a cruisy crowd of men with pick-up lines like, 'How big's your dick?'

The very first night I met a very nice person from the British Armed Services. I warmed to him, especially when he sat beside me, bought me drinks and asked to see me again. In three days he was 'madly in love'. In those days I rarely, if ever, used the word 'love', even though he pushed me to say it. Being chased by someone so attractive was flattering. Being courted felt wonderful. He was spending heaps of money on me, buying my affection. We had a whirlwind series of romantic weekends at the Chateau and in Rotorua.

One night, in a relaxed pub setting, we talked about Our Future. He was returning to England and persuaded me to follow him. I didn't know if I was doing the right thing or not. All my friends, except for one, said, 'Go for it!' The one exception advised, 'If you don't love him, don't go.' In the end, the deciding factor was how good it felt being with someone compared to the prospect of being alone again.

I told my grandmother I was going overseas to join this guy. She said, 'That's wonderful, when am I going to meet him?' She had no problem with it. I took him over to her place and she sent me on a walk while they got to know each other. By this time there was a general awareness of AIDS, and both my grandmother and my parents warned me about it.

As soon as I got on that plane to go to the UK I knew I'd made a mistake. Even as the plane landed I was working out how to go home. I landed in the UK on April Fool's Day, and had three days in London, during which I saw Larry Kramer's play, one of the very first dramas about AIDS, called *The Lonely Heart*. Five minutes into it, I started crying. I now think it was a premonition of my own HIV status.

After arriving at my boyfriend's place I had a false appendix attack. I mentioned that I was gay to the GP, who informed my boyfriend's superiors. Security came around, arrested my boyfriend and questioned the neighbours. They tried to search the house. He said we were flatmates and he was merely reciprocating a New Zealand friendship.

We were being watched. I couldn't go anywhere. I had to move out of his bed. I couldn't use the phone — it was tapped. They intercepted our mail. This surveillance destroyed whatever affection we had for each other, and nine months after leaving New Zealand I returned, a wreck.

Still, he was the one big love of my life. I didn't contact him when I was diagnosed HIV+, but phoned when I passed through London on my way to represent New Zealand at the sixth International Conference for People Living with AIDS and HIV, which was held in Madrid. He nearly fell off his chair when I said, 'It's Michael Hay here.' There was this incredibly long silence. I told him why I was passing through London. I was really pleased that I called. It was like laying a demon to rest.

Back in New Zealand I retrained as a computer analyst, mainly because I heard the money was very good. Once trained, I slipped easily into middle management, but I was no good as a boss. I couldn't tell people off. But for once I was making money and, on a whim, bought a bach at Rotorua.

In 1988, the week of my thirty-sixth birthday, I got my HIV+ diagnosis. It was my third HIV test, and I expected the result to be positive. I had already had some telling symptoms — night sweats and swollen glands. The GP called my parents, trying to find me. He called me at work and told me my results over the phone. I kept calm. I finished the day's work and went to see my parents.

My mistake was not to go straight to them as soon as I took the GP's call. Instead I called Mum from work. She begged me to tell her the result, but I said, 'No, I'll tell you this evening.' Both Mum and Dad were in heavy shock by the time I got there and confirmed their worst fears. I sat in the living room and even then, after all the years of support they'd given me — they'd always supported me, from the day I came out to them — I still couldn't talk about my feelings. They weren't sure how to express their feelings for me. I misinterpreted their caution as a sign they didn't care about me, which was completely wrong. It's taken me several years to put myself in their shoes and appreciate just how much they have loved me and supported me over the years.

Everyone takes their HIV diagnosis differently. This may sound strange but, for me, it was a good diagnosis. To me HIV equalled AIDS equalled DEATH. I thought that within a month I'd be dead and my whole miserable life would be over. I stayed away from the counsellors at the Burnett Clinic. 'They'll just make me face being gay,' I thought.

I quit my job. My workmates, I'm sure, suspected what was wrong, and gave me a very nice send-off. I retreated to Rotorua to die. Whenever I saw something in the news-papers about a new AIDS cure, my heart would sink. I don't particularly believe in God but if I did I would have said He was punishing me by giving me a long life, by making me a long-term survivor of HIV. I still hadn't got what I wanted: death. That's how I was thinking then.

I was brought back to reality, and back to life, really, with the arrival of lots of bills. GST bills. Tax bills. I had been living on disability insurances and tax credits. I sold my bach and rented a house on the shores of Lake Rotorua.

I started 1989 by attending a Kübler Ross 'Life, Death and Transition' workshop in Taupo. It was for community nurses working with the terminally ill, and for people facing a terminal illness. This workshop was the beginning of my healing. I watched and listened to people talk about their feelings. I had to hear their tragic, dreadful stories. I found it hard not to be affected by their grief and anger. As my emotions came to the surface I fell to pieces. I froze. I couldn't move out of my chair. With the help of the others, I finally identified the very small boy inside me who needed to be looked after.

I started to reach out to other HIV+ people and came upon a copy of *Collective Thinking*, the magazine put out by HIV+ people in New Zealand. That April I wrote to the editor, Daniel Fielding. 'I'm here in Rotorua, what can I do?' Before I knew it, he'd sent me to a meeting in Auckland where I was voted on to the board of the New Zealand Aids Foundation. It was like going from 0 to 200k in 20 seconds.

Although I'm no longer on the board of the Foundation — I resigned due to differences of opinion with other board members — I am still very much involved in the fight against HIV/AIDS and in helping people living with HIV/AIDS in New Zealand. I'm on the National Executive of the New Zealand Persons Living With Aids Union. I'm a co-opted member on the Executive Committee of the New Zealand Venereological Society. I'm on the Public Health Commission's Sexual Health and HIV/AIDS Advisory Committee, and a member of the New Zealand Scientific Advisory Committee on AIDS. I do HIV/AIDS education in the Bay of Plenty, and work for the Bay Area AIDS Support Services — something I set up. I'm on the Programme Advisory Committee for Humanities at the Polytechnic here in Rotorua. I now edit *Collective Thinking*, the largest HIV+ magazine in the country. I'm not a doctor, I've no medical training, yet I'm one of this country's most knowledgeable people about AIDS, HIV and the treatments thereof.

It sounds surprising, I know, but in a strange way I can say that HIV is the most positive thing that ever happened to me. In the beginning I thought, 'HIV equals immediate death.' I now see how being HIV+ has empowered — God, I hate that word! — me and made it okay for me to address so many issues within my life. It started me freeing myself of my personal inhibitions and fully realising my potential. It's allowed me to leave my mark on New Zealand, because copies of *Collective Thinking* are in the archives, and people will be looking at them long into the future.

I regret not having participated more fully in the gay community over the years. Even now I'm always happier with straight crowds. Put a few gay men together and they have common points of reference that mean nothing to me. I'm still very much a heterosexual queer.

I also regret that I've never had a mutually satisfying, intimate relationship. It's not in my destiny to have one. My love hides itself away, torn between 'gregarious' and 'got to be safe'.

In the past couple of years I've become very close to my parents, my brothers and their families again. We've made up the distance and let go of old angers. They've been so very wonderful to me. My being ill has given them the opportunity to show their love for me, and given me the opportunity to acknowledge their love and show mine in return.

My big fault is I still don't value myself enough. I still don't know why people like me. My one hope is that before I die I'll know who the real Michael is, not the fabricated pieces I put up on show for other people.

Postscript: In January 1995, although very ill with various complications from his HIV infection, Michael travelled up from Rotorua to Auckland to see his family and to receive an award at the AIDS Foundation Media Awards for his excellent work helping people living with HIV/AIDS.

He and I went over the final revisions of his life history at this time. He was staying with his parents, Alan and Molly, who, with Michael's brothers and their families, were caring for him 24 hours a day. It was an exhausting, stressful experience for them all, but one, I know from experience, that has deep personal rewards.

Michael learned to depend upon his parents and his brothers for his most intimate care. Through their daily struggles together he realised how much his family loved him. This knowledge made him very happy. Despite being debilitated, Michael was very much at ease with his family, cheerful and up-beat. It was a privilege to see them united together.

Michael died 2 February 1995, in Rotorua, cared for by his friends and his family. Shortly thereafter, a grand movie premiere of *Priscilla, Queen of the Desert* was held as a memorial to Michael and to raise funds to continue his work. Molly says it was a marvellous evening. The city closed off the main street and the mayor, civic dignitaries, Michael's family and friends partied well into the night, and raised lots of money for HIV/AIDS education in the Bay area. It was a wonderful finale. Michael's ashes lie beneath a beautiful rhododendron tree on a tranquil Rotorua hillside where, I'm certain, he rests in peace.

Coimm Macrae [1]

I was born in the last year of the war, one month premature. I seemed to have been in a hurry, for the first and only time in my life. My mother tells me that, apart from being very small, I wasn't any bother. I like to joke that I was built within the standards of the War Economy Agreement.

By chance I was born in Hamilton, for my father, then in the Air Force, was temporarily posted to Te Rapa. We returned to Dunedin a couple of months after my birth, so I suppose it's only right and proper that I consider myself a Dunediner because that's where I was conceived, supposed to be born, and where I spent the first half of my life.

My early childhood was not unusual in any sense. Like many New Zealanders I began life in a state house. After about six years my parents managed to buy a house nearby, a 1930s bungalow by a golf links, right on the edge of Dunedin. It was the only house in the street besides the clubhouse. One thing I really remember from my childhood was that I had no peers or companions living anywhere near. I was isolated in a way. I mean, I could walk to school easily enough — it was only three-quarters of a mile — but the nearest houses were two or three blocks away. I suspect this

1 Coimm Macrae is a pseudonym

had quite a bearing on my shyness, actually. If you've got kids over the fence it makes a hell of a difference.

I have two sisters, four and 10 years younger than me. I remember being sent off to some Boy Scout camp in something of a rush, and coming home to find I had another sister. I had a brother, too, born two years after me, who didn't survive more than a few weeks. His head was severely damaged in delivery by what I can only call unforgivable medical mismanagement. My mother has never quite got over it, because there was nothing wrong with him. She tells me that I was most distraught for some time as well. I suspect this gap in my life has never been filled.

We had a very stable family life, with frequent contact with my cousins, aunts, uncles, etc. My father, like his father before him, is an engineer and managed a large garage. One of the highlights of my boyhood was when he got called out to major motor accidents. Dad's speciality was rescuing vehicles that other people wouldn't even attempt to reach. They were *the* salvage firm in that part of Otago, and we used to range all over the place. For example, he'd say to me on Friday, 'We're getting up early tomorrow, to go and rescue a grader in Roxburgh.' I used to enjoy these little bits of excitement. Although he always encouraged me to be handy, my father had no notion of my becoming an engineer. He said, 'One member of the family with dirty fingernails is quite enough.' Little did he know that I would take up printing later in life!

The family was church oriented. My father was an elder, a lay reader and organist of the local Union parish. At eight I became a chorister and have only recently given it up. Church music has always been a central core to my life.

When I facilitate workshops on sexuality — a fairly regular

assignment that's evolved quite naturally out of my medical speciality — I'm always intrigued about the age people report as the time of their sexual awakening. For most people it's at, or about, the time of puberty. It wasn't for me. My sexuality began at the age of eight, not because I was seduced — I was far too shy for that — but because I discovered masturbation purely by accident.

At that time school textbooks were in short supply and we often had to share. One day, sharing with a classmate, I sat with the desk leg between my legs, and my penis got caught between the desk leg and my own leg. If you put pressure on an intact penis, the glans will move within the foreskin. In this situation mine did so, and gave me this surge of sensation that I couldn't quite understand. When I reached down to find out why, I discovered that fingers did the same thing. I've always had a very sensitive penis and even now can reach orgasm, with optimal stimulation, within 15 to 20 seconds.

Playing with your foreskin, causing the penis to swell up and stiffen dramatically, would frighten any boy. But at eight years of age, who do you talk to? I worried intensely about what was happening. However, it was too nice to stop and it became a daily event. Many nights I would fall asleep out of sheer exhaustion because I had probably had eight, 10 or 12 orgasms, one after the other in quick succession, without losing my erection. No wonder I became quite addicted to it! All pre-pubescent boys have the capacity to enjoy unlimited orgasms, and the annoying thing about the arrival of puberty is the loss of this orgasmic potential, which disappears shortly after ejaculation commences. I was very upset about that.

What was sad was the lack of sex education, which meant

I developed the most extraordinary guilt and concern. I really felt that one day my penis would drop off, out of abuse or whatever. There were dark mutterings about 'self-abuse'. The Boy Scout manual didn't help, because it told you that if you did dirty things like that, hair grew on the palms of the hands or you went blind or insane. If you smoked as well, it was certain you'd be a physical wreck by the time you were 25. My *Cole's Funny Picture Book* had this picture of a healthy youth next to the lurid portrait of a youth who had smoked and indulged in self-abuse: his tongue stuck out, he slathered at the mouth and he was dissipated beyond belief — in other words he was a shattered wreck. Now I don't think I was told this classic Victorian belief directly, but I certainly worried a great deal about it happening to me. It didn't stop me, nevertheless.

Intermediate school was an excellent introduction to high school. I went from a new and struggling primary school to a mature intermediate school with a good social mix, drawn from several other schools. The teachers were brilliant, both in the classroom and in the technical subjects. Gardening and manual classes were obligatory for boys, while girls went off to the cooking classes and home science.

When I turned 12 my parents must have decided — I'm guessing here, because I haven't really discussed this with them — that I needed drawing out of my shell of shyness, so they sent me off to a Bible class camp on the Taieri Plains. It was like being sent into the army, I suppose. The accommodation was a number of huts. Each had six bunks, for five boys and a chaperone. There was a central main building and a decrepit swimming pool half-filled with debris, including wrecked farm machinery sticking out of very brackish water.

On the first night we were sent to bed long before the adults, who stayed up planning the week. The four other boys in my chalet were more outgoing than me, so I clambered into a top bunk and lay down and watched what they were up to. They decided to get up to some sexual games — we were all at the age of curiosity: a bit of 'show and tell' and mutual fondling. I was very intrigued. Firstly, it was a revelation to discover that I wasn't the only boy playing with his cock. I was delighted to find out that other boys did the same thing and that it wasn't freakish behaviour on my part. Secondly, I was astonished to see they did it with the tips of their penises bare. I never did that because my own glans was far too sensitive and I never drew my foreskin back when masturbating.

One of them suddenly noticed me watching and said, 'Why isn't he involved? There are no spectators in this game.' I was forcibly removed from my bunk and stripped. Much to their amazement they had never seen a cock like mine before. Suddenly it ceased to be a game of mutual masturbation and became a case of, 'Let's examine this strange cock.'

I was petrified, of course, because it was then I realised they didn't have any moveable skin over the head of their penises at all. They didn't understand the difference either. My foreskin was stripped back forcibly to see whether I was normal underneath, which I was. None of us could understand why I had this flap of skin. The next day the news I had a deformed penis was all around the camp, and for the whole week I was subject to clandestine grabbing by boys much bigger than me, taken around the back of a bush, then stripped to see this strange cock. I was a small kid and this was very traumatic. I became the fall guy of the camp, I suppose. On one occasion, hotly pursued by a posse of bigger boys intent, they said, on throwing me into that terrible pool if my penis was as deformed as rumoured, I ran to the caretaker's house where I appealed to an adult for protection, because I was really scared of being seriously hurt. The response I got was, 'Face up to it like a man!' and I was thrown out to the wolves again. Fortunately I was borne off bodily for just another stripping and rough penile inspection. I recall being really terrified by the possibility of serious bodily harm.

I arrived home in a far worse state than I had gone, and my parents couldn't work out why the camp hadn't done me any good. To this day I've never told them what happened, and it took me a long time to get over this experience. It was also the beginning of a life-long abhorrence of circumcision and my near-obsessional need to discover someone like myself.

The next year, 1957, I started at high school. Around April of that year a good friend in the class, also aged 13, talked me into a little bit of hanky-panky. I can't remember how he managed to do this, because I was still very shy. I would have expected to have said 'No!' But I trusted him and somehow or other he talked me into going off with him to a secluded spot in the school grounds where he suggested that we explore one another.

I must have just started puberty, for my cock had only just begun to grow and I had not yet ejaculated. He was much more advanced than me, and I was impressed with his size and so on. But like the boys at the camp, he was cut and I didn't know how to handle a cut cock. There were no moving parts and I couldn't understand why the skin was tight on the shaft when his penis was erect. I was reluctant to touch his bare glans, knowing how sensitive my own glans was. He explained carefully how to slide the shaft skin up against his corona and back down. This movement was very restricted but had the appropriate effect, because he eventually reached orgasm. I had heard of ejaculation but not seen it, and I was fascinated by his fountain of semen.

When he began to handle me, he said, 'What have we got here?' I was a revelation to him, too. He was puzzled by my 'excess' of skin, which he'd never seen before. I still couldn't explain why I was different. I knew I was the same as my father, and I thought, well, it must be a freakish genetic thing that exists in the family. He didn't make any derogatory comments, which I feared he might.

He then proceeded to play with me and rolled my foreskin on and off my glans, something I was not in the habit of doing because my extreme sensitivity required only gentle movement of the foreskin to achieve rapid orgasm. Anyway, things went well and the sensation, which was quite different and very pleasant, ended, to my amazement, with my first ejaculation. Because I hadn't really any idea what was going to happen I was grateful that my first ejaculation wasn't alone. My semen was tinged a little with blood. The fact my friend had been through the same experience months before, and could say, 'Don't worry about that, that always happens the first time,' was very reassuring. If it had happened while I'd been alone, it might have rekindled the fears that all this self-abuse was really damaging. It was great that this experienced friend was able to say, 'Don't worry. This is exactly what you must expect.' He was also quite delighted and said, 'Fancy that! Your first shooting with me.'

A few months later another classmate interrupted cricket practice and suggested that we should go off and play around. I quickly discovered that he was cut too. By this stage, having noticed other classmates, I concluded that no one else had a foreskin. But his reaction on seeing me was, 'God! You're lucky. You've still got your foreskin.' I asked him what he meant and he showed me the scar on his cock, explaining everything about foreskins and the fact he'd been circumcised the year before, at the age of 12, under false pretences. He'd gone to have a tonsillectomy and came out hurting at each end, more or less, which annoyed him intensely. Like me, he'd started sexual life early and knew what it was like, before and after. 'You don't know how lucky you are,' he said. Later on, when I was back with my first friend, I was able to point out the scar on his cock which he'd never noticed before. I was able to say, 'You also had a foreskin, once upon a time.'

That was the turning point. But of course, like all curious boys, I had to find out if there was anyone else like me around. I must have checked out a lot of cocks over the next few years. I discovered you don't have to undress a boy, or get to the point of actually fondling his genitals, to learn whether he's cut or intact. In the rough and tumble of school play, there was a good deal of wrestling where genital grasping was quite common. It was an acceptable practice, and probably still is, amongst boys of that age; you gained an advantage if you could get a handful of genitals. If your opponent wouldn't give up, or was being too rough in my case, you could give his genitals a squeeze. To see if a boy was circumcised or not, I simply had to give the tip of the penis a gentle squeeze. If a foreskin was present, the tip would withdraw because the glans automatically slips inside the foreskin. So I learned instantly whether he was cut or intact. Without actually having sex with them all, I knew the circumcision status of nearly every boy in my class.

There were over 750 boys at my high school and I did not discover any who were intact. I now know that this is not surprising, considering that Dunedin is a medical school city and circumcision was the 'in' thing between about 1940 and 1955, when New Zealand's circumcision rate was very high indeed. In fact, in Dunedin it probably reached more than 90 per cent. So the chance of my finding anyone else like me was really rare. My mother says the reason I was never circumcised is family tradition. Apparently she had to make a very strong point indeed that I was to be left untouched. The doctors came by every day and said, 'We'd better fix him before you go.' 'Don't you dare,' she said. In fact, she had me moved from the nursery into her room to protect me.

I am grateful for being intact. But I know from my counselling work, and my studies of the United States experience, that some intact men consider they would have preferred to be cut, in order to fit in with everybody else. It did cross my mind, at first, but it didn't take too much intellectual effort to realise that my high level of sensitivity, and the pleasure I got from sex, was directly related to the possession of a foreskin. I only had to observe the boys I had sex with at high school to realise that their sexual response was nothing like mine. There are certain things you can do with an intact penis that you can't do with a circumcised one, which is simply not easy to handle. Intact men seem to have sensations that are more intense.

I've only ever had one derogatory comment from a sex partner regarding my foreskin. In my early teens one friend said he thought it smelt a bit, so I became very conscious of hygiene.

I didn't come across another intact male until I was 16. He was a country boy, the son of the local grocer near our holiday home in Central Otago. He took me off walking one day to see some of the gold-mine relics, and in the process decided I was fit for seduction. He was beautifully intact, which was a great joy to both of us, actually, for he'd fully expected me to be a city slicker. Unfortunately he joined the Armed Services soon after and I never saw him again. However, it was nice to find a kindred anatomical spirit at last.

Some people say you can pick the time at which you realise you're gay. I'm not so sure, but I always knew I was different in some way. Not just because I was intact. There was something else different about me. Ever since I can remember I'd always been fascinated with other men's bodies. Looking at other men, I've always focused on their face first and then their crotch. Sexually, there'd been plenty of schoolboy stuff from the ages of 13 to 17. But by 17 all my classmates had left me behind and got involved with girls in one way or another, and I seemed to be the only one in my class who hadn't. This is when I really came to the realisation that I was gay. From that point onwards, Dunedin was a very lonely city for me.

It became even lonelier when I went to university and lost the immediate contact of my schoolmates. I didn't spend enough time with any one group to develop a close rapport, being just one of 20,000 other students. I don't think I've never been more lonely, physically, than I was as an undergraduate. There were no gay clubs. I remember hearing someone say that all the queers met in a certain coffee bar in Lower Downing Street. Well, I sat in that place until all hours, drinking coffee until it came out of my ears, not seeing anybody or anything. My love life was going nowhere. One or two old school friends were still interested in playing around, but only on a very infrequent basis. Sexually the years from 17 to 24 were a complete desert, including the year I spent in the Navy. In the Navy, of course, it was a no-no. I only ever had one gay experience, when another rating tried to touch me up in the showers. Although I was enchanted by the idea, I was absolutely petrified of the consequences. So I talked him out of it. Indeed, it wasn't until I went to Wellington, at the age of 23, to study for my professional qualifications that things changed.

In Wellington I sang in St Peter's Church choir and played the carillon. Thursday nights I always arrived late for choir practice, because I had the prior carillon recital to attend. One Thursday I slipped into the bass stalls and noticed a new face on the other side of the chancel. It was a new chorister, fresh from England, and he was staring at me with a very puzzled look on his face. Later I found out why — he was very surprised at anyone arriving late. Having already been introduced to everyone else, he was also surprised, and disappointed, to discover that every male chorister was straight. He could tell if you were gay or not by reading your eyes. He was absolutely 100 per cent at this and he looked in the eyes of every chorister when he was introduced. Not a flicker. 'Oh dear, another straight,' he thought, and by the time I arrived he'd given up on finding any gay men. Seeing me across the chancel (we're talking 40 feet), he thought, 'Well, well.' That's why he was staring at me so intently. He was trying to read my eyes.

If there's one thing I've never been able to disguise, it's my eyes. You'd think, having been in the service and lived a fairly underground life, that I'd be reasonably hard to pick as gay. I don't fit into the classic queen mould at all. My wrists aren't flippy or anything like that. So I'm always surprised at how many times someone's said to me, 'Oh yes, I always knew you were gay.'

I didn't realise *he* was gay. I had no idea about the gay scene in Wellington. I had a circle of good friends — all straight — and had resigned myself to the idea that perhaps someone special might pop out of the blue, but I wasn't out looking every night. About a month later, he and I went to a party at Waikanae with some straight friends and we fetched up in a caravan together because the cottage was so full of people. Realising how shy I was he eventually, and very carefully, made a pass at me, and we became close friends.

He introduced me to Wellington's gay scene. It had only taken him about a week to find out where everything was happening. I'd spent months and months in the damn city and didn't know a thing. If it wasn't for him, I don't know what would have happened for me. It's sad to look back on those seven wasted years.

I didn't actually fall deeply in love until I was 28, when I was in Canada, where I taught bacteriology and bio-chemistry in Victoria, British Colombia, for nearly three years. Falling in love was just as Barbara Cartland describes it: Love at first sight.

It happened in the cathedral in Victoria on Christmas Eve 1971. We came out from the midnight service to find it had snowed while we were inside — my first white Christmas. I went around to the choir room, to be introduced to the director of music and others. Everyone was absolutely wonderful and made me very welcome. Chris was busy putting all the music away and he came in after the others. When we were introduced he looked up into my eyes —

he's a little shorter than I am — and it was an instant transfer, a bit like R2D2 from *Star Wars* plugging into a computer terminal. I looked into this man's pale blue eyes and I was lost. Stunned speechless. I couldn't reply. I couldn't understand what was happening. I just felt that I was being read like a book. I already knew that Chris, who's a few years older than me, and very experienced in the gay scene and life in general, was in a relationship with the director of music. 'There's no way that he's available,' I thought, and that was that.

Six months later I went to stay with him overnight and he said, 'Well, you can sleep on the couch or you can sleep with me.' Looking at the semi-circular couch, I replied, 'I'll sleep with you, thank you.' Of course, for those six months I'd been gradually falling in love with him all the way. Our relationship became extremely intense, so much so that we could communicate telepathically. Now, as a scientist, I've always had quite a bit of trouble believing in telepathy, but when you're involved yourself it becomes really mind-boggling.

Our relationship was not destined to be. He reconciled with his lover and I eventually returned to New Zealand. Within six months his lover accepted a job at Cornell University, so they broke up for good and the man I loved has lived alone ever since. This is one of the tragedies in my life. If only I'd stayed in Canada, he may have been mine.

I had no intentions of leaving Canada. I was absolutely charmed with Canadians, who had helped me completely overcome my shyness. They just wouldn't tolerate it and, for the first time in my life, I became socially adept and was a reasonable party animal. You discover you're a different person overseas. Without even trying, you become exotic and entertaining. Suddenly you have this charming accent and you interact far more easily. In Canada a few people lusted after me, and this was quite nice because it never happened to me in New Zealand, probably because I'd always had a totally different aura at home.

My return from Canada was precipitated by a close call with cancer. One morning, in the shower, I experienced a dreadful pain in one testis. With my pathology background I realised precisely what it was — a testicular cancer. 'Well,' I thought, 'it's been a short life but a sweet one.' My doctor sent me straight to a specialist, who operated on me next day. I was fortunate because they discovered my cancer wasn't fatally malignant — at the time, most of these cancers were absolutely deadly. The physicians and my surgeon said, 'You've got to go through intensive radiotherapy. You may be very unwell. Because you're a bachelor, with no one to care for you here, it's best you go back to New Zealand to be in the care of your family.' I took their advice and came back, but have always wished I hadn't because my illness wasn't, in fact, as bad as all that, although I did go down from eleven and a half stone to nine stone during radiotherapy, and looked more dead than alive for six months. I've had no problems since, so I must consider myself very lucky.

After Canada, New Zealand came as a shock. We're all very reserved here. It's quite different in North America. I loved my first visit to a Californian gay bar where, within five minutes, some fellow walked up, said he fancied me and asked, 'Your place or mine?' Compare this to the first gay party I went to in Wellington when I got back from Canada. People spent all night circling one another, too frightened to make the first move, for fear of rejection. Several men, myself included, went home alone because they couldn't bring themselves to make the first approach. In the States or Canada, if you fancy someone, you just say so. If they're not available, they say straight back, without any nastiness at all, 'Sorry, I'm otherwise spoken for', or whatever. You don't waste any time. In New Zealand you wait the whole night, before making a move. If he says 'No', it's too late to ask anyone else.

In 1973, the year I came back, I took up a post at Victoria University, but I was unsettled and moved around quite a bit. In 1977 I returned full time to the Navy. In 1981 I became a research associate at Auckland Hospital. And in 1984 I moved to National Women's Hospital, where I stayed for nine years until leaving to become a full-time student at Auckland Medical School, where I have been reading for a Masters degree in anatomy. I don't know what I'll do when I finish that; I may get back into teaching again. I don't wish to go back into the Health Service which is, I think, a very unhealthy environment, for it certainly didn't do my health any good.

I'm not very active in music now. I recently retired as a chorister, because the practice nights clashed with other things. I'm a keen printer and bookbinder, and gardening is a passion I've had since a teenager. On my way home from high school I used to cycle past this nursery. Always a rather curious individual, I used to stop, to gather my breath and look at whatever they were doing. One day I fell to talking to one of the partners who said, 'Well, if you're that curious, come by on Saturday and I'll show you round.' So I did. He said, 'What do you know?' 'Not much,' I replied. To which he said, 'Today's task is to take cuttings off all the stock fuchsias and prune the rest.' That was the beginning. I worked at that nursery all the years I was at school and got a very good horticultural training. I had a flourishing garden at home. I've always been fascinated by propagation — not that I always succeed. I now belong to Auckland's burgeoning gay gardening group, which has gay, lesbian and bisexual members. It's an absolutely wonderful group.

Having spent so much time away from home in the past, it was great to settle down at last. It's a very real privilege to share one's life in every respect with another, and to have done so with my partner for 13 years now is especially wonderful. We met through the efforts of another couple whom we have christened 'The Marriage Bureau'. We also joke that our partnership is an 'arranged marriage'. Having a home of our own, complete with pussy cat, garden, etc., makes for happiness and commitment. I must say, life is never dull for a gay man who has good friends.

Victor
van Wetering

I was born in 1961, in Auckland, Wednesday's child, the middle son in a family of five boys. My childhood was fairly idyllic. I had a very supportive family, and I got on well with my parents and my brothers, though there were inevitable conflicts natural to a family of five boys. I've always identified more easily with people outside my own age group. Whether this is because of my social interaction or conditioning related to sexual identity, I don't know. I suspect it's just me!

I didn't have any real inclination of my sexual identity until my teens, but I remember a few early incidents which signalled something. I can recall watching a man — he was probably an adolescent, but he seemed very old to me at the time — walking down the street where I used to live, and being very attracted by, of all things, his bare feet! I also remember obvious taboos about being gay, but they were rarely enunciated in depth until secondary school, where it became clear that I was not one of the mob.

Then, I thought this sense of difference was because I was an individual and generally more intelligent and articulate than most of my classmates. Certainly, asserting my 'individuality' regularly resulted in conflict or isolation. I went to a Catholic school and I would regularly challenge the religious studies teacher and really hack off the rest of the class, who would have preferred a quieter time. I was also the first boy at my college to take typing — and as if to add insult to injury, I came first in class! I played some sport, but opted out of rugby when it became obvious that life as a forward was too dull, brutal or violent to be considered sensible. Some people might consider nuzzling between hairy thighs in a scrum great fun for a burgeoning gay boy, but, believe me, it just isn't that exciting.

The consequences of these sort of actions were compounded because the priests teaching us were Dutch and, with a Dutch surname, I was perceived to be aligned with them rather than my social group. Perhaps this identified me, in my classmates' minds, as being on the side of the Establishment. Whatever the reasons, I was quite badly bullied at secondary school and had a particularly unhappy fourth form year. I now realise that many of my classmates would have picked up signals that I was gay more readily than I did myself. I remember two boys in my art class who did identify as gay and were isolated, but they drew friends around them more successfully, and managed to be happy together, because they understood how they were different.

My college was co-ed from the third form and I found the girls more approachable than the boys, and those friendships provided a certain level of sanctuary. This probably also distanced me from male classmates, but it seemed like a good trade-off at the time. I remember attempting to make out with some of the girls, but it was all pretty clumsy and nothing came of it.

I have always had a very close relationship with my parents; my mother is a great advocate of freedom and my father is a very demonstrative, warm person. But, during my adolescence, I grew quite combative and put real distance between them, particularly between my father and myself. Maybe it's what Germaine Greer talks about, that at a certain age boys distance themselves from their parents to reinforce the fact that they're developing as men and need to make the break. I know that I was quite difficult during my adolescence, and while I can't attribute all of that to my emerging sexuality, it was a factor.

Around this time I acquired another clue that I was 'different'. I remember lying down on the living-room floor to watch television. I lay on my side, curled up in a half-foetal position, while my brothers leaned back on their elbows, half sitting up. Our body language was completely different, and I thought, 'Well, that's interesting.' Increasingly, I was developing a clearer idea of the markers which identified me as different, but I still didn't know what the source of the difference was. Fortunately, I remained relatively free of conventional Catholic guilt trips, mainly because my parents had a left-wing, liberal view of religion. But I find the associations between guilt and homosexuality fascinating and the number of Catholic boys who are gay startling.

I finished secondary school an academic success but feeling something of a social failure. I went straight to teachers' college. Some friends recommended I not pass straight from one educational institution to another, but for me it was great. I was the second youngest student teacher of my intake, and I suddenly found myself sampling a menu of social and academic options that I'd never had available before. I became involved in lots of courses, student politics and editing the college magazine. I had immense energy; I was like a pinball, racing round the campus, doing everything I could and enjoying the huge variety of people and talent around me.

At teachers' college I had a few relationships, some with women and some with men, but they were largely fumbled attempts. I'm not implying that the college had courses in sexual intimacy, but I was lucky that, at 17, I had the opportunity to explore these options.

During my second year I went flatting and found myself getting involved with people emotionally rather than physically. Two of my dearest friends hail from those times. We graduated together in 1980 and remain very close. It was about this time that I began to tell my family about my emerging sexual identity. I remember explaining to my mother that I might be bisexual. It was classic, of course, telling *her* first, so she could decide when to tell Dad, and saying *bisexual* because it was a 'softer' option than pure homosexuality. At the time I was genuinely confused, with most received messages telling me: 'You should go for that', while I was thinking: 'No, I'd rather go for this.' Mum wrote me a great letter, acknowledging that I might be influenced by the gay people I knew and respected, but that I should consider the difficulties they faced. At the time we accepted the notion of 'choice', but it has since become the natural way to be.

After graduating I started teaching near Auckland. Certain residents in the area, which I dubbed 'the insular peninsula', deduced that I was gay and made life quite difficult. Their children would shout anti-gay comments across the playground at me. But I was lucky because my headmaster and immediate boss were, like me, both new to the school and very supportive.

I had my first intense sexual relationship with a man that

year, and it was wonderful — a revelation, an explosion of excitement.

My next teaching job was a two-year stint at Petone Central, and it was during this period that I began to come out. I was very hesitant about it. Apart from being reluctant to identify with the gay community, which at the time was extremely turned in on itself, there had been a scandal, some years earlier, when a government minister was smeared by the anti-gay innuendo of then-Opposition leader Robert Muldoon. I myself had entertained political aspirations, and what became known as 'the Moyle Affair' impressed me as a cautionary tale about the damage of disclosure. It had a profound effect upon me. It took a long time, and the evolution of greater tolerance in New Zealand society, before I could contemplate being publicly out or acknowledge that part of my character.

The Petone years were good: it's a working-class, multicultural area and I learnt something valuable there. In my first year I pitted myself against the kids, but in the next I went with their energy and had a superb year.

Then, in 1984, I went to Dannevirke. I don't know what possessed me exactly, except that in those days primary teachers had to apply widely for work and they went where the jobs were. This 'permanent' position turned out to be very temporary. Dannevirke was your typical redneck town and moving there proved to be a bruising mistake, especially after my headmaster told members of the local white golf club he had a poofter on the staff. It did rather damage relationships with the parents of the children I taught.

I've left a lot of that year behind me. But one thing I learnt about small-town New Zealand is that it isn't divided just between the tolerant and intolerant; it's also divided on race.

I was very fortunate to make friends there who became whanau — a passport to an alternative way of survival, a remedy for thoughts of suicide. I remember driving home after a bad day at school and considering driving off a bridge. But I decided instead to see the Haurakis, my neighbours. Paul played great blues guitar, Heather always made me welcome and their son, Santana, was an entrancing four-year-old. The three became my second family and we still keep in touch. Paul was also my link with Dannevirke's 'Maori' pub and a circle of staunch friends who were pleasantly surprised to see a teacher in their midst, one who didn't wear walk-shorts and sandals or share the disdain reserved for the local Maori by the white majority.

I left teaching and Dannevirke at the end of 1984, returning to Wellington to complete my degree and to pursue writing. Victoria was a good campus for gay people, and conducive to productivity: in one year I partied, worked part-time, passed 48 credits and wrote about 50 pieces for various publications.

University also furnished me with a few partners who helped clarify my sexual predilections, but no one I met set the heart racing — though a fair amount of blood rushed elsewhere. Eventually I tired of the largesse my body prompted and recognised the fallacy that sexual freedom means fulfilment.

After varsity, I completed the Wellington Polytechnic journalism course and joined the *Evening Post* as television writer. A couple of gay guys there helped my confidence and my coming out. They reinforced the fact that to be out didn't mean you had to merge into a tribalistic 'scene' which, then at least, didn't readily accommodate individuality, though it provided support and a sexual smorgasbord.

In 1985 I met Kevarnos. The chemistry, and my boredom with short flings, persuaded me to go for the relationship and he moved in — the start of a four-year partnership. We made a home together and were sold on the idea of being a couple.

I find it hard to detail what the relationship was about out of a sense of loyalty and some guilt over it failing, and because it genuinely took over my life. Kevarnos had been damaged when he was younger and, in some ways, I appropriated a sense of responsibility for that. In other ways I feel I let him down. We loved each other very much but didn't communicate well and, even as the conflicts became more common, we were loath to let go.

My parents weren't surprised when we broke up, but they never distinguished between the hospitality they offered Kevarnos and my brothers' girlfriends. I still care about him and I'm pleased that he's found happiness with another. It still matters to me how he is.

With the relationship over, Wellington and my job held less appeal, so I spent eight months travelling: Bali, Thailand, Malaysia, India, Nepal, Turkey and most of Europe. I arrived in London on Christmas Eve 1990 for a reunion with my brothers, the first time in five years we'd been together. It was a defining moment. The competition that had dom-inated our adolescence, that sometimes made the family home seem so small, was gone. We'd all made our own way as individuals, adults. The bad 'history' didn't matter; we were clan in a foreign country and there was space for each of us.

I started teaching in London the day the Gulf War began. It was a fascinating time and place to be working there. The children I taught at this Anglican church school in the

East End were predominantly Muslim; the school was directly opposite Murdoch's Wapping plant, where pitched battles between picketers and police had occurred; and my class wrote an opera about working children in Victorian times and performed it in a nearby renovated music hall which was the site of Charlie Chaplin's first London performances.

Later that year I began work as a press officer for the Terrence Higgins Trust, Europe's largest AIDS organisation. This served as an apprenticeship of sorts for my later work for the New Zealand AIDS Foundation. In Britain, a draconian social environment inspires radicalism in the large but diversely 'branded' gay community. The government is uncomfortable with HIV and AIDS issues, so it slips agencies money to produce safe-sex materials about activities which ministers don't even want to think about! In New Zealand we have the reverse situation with, legislatively speaking, one of the world's best environments for gay people and people affected by HIV.

I enjoyed my work for these organisations tremendously. As a journalist, I understood the needs of reporters and researchers who would seek comment or information, and I was able to provide them with ideas which helped secure advantageous stories for my employers and, most importantly, for those affected by HIV. Britain's media provided more of a challenge, and more hostility, but I was adept at breaking down the 'us-and-them' mentality. 'Yes,' I would say, 'safe sex *is* hard to negotiate. For instance, if you had unsafe sex in an affair, how would you then introduce the subject, or condoms, into your regular relationship?' Fortunately English newspapers like the *Guardian* and the *Independent* proved more than equal to the 'guilty victim' mentality of the right, which equated HIV and AIDS as suitable punishment for perverted homosexuals.

In New Zealand a generally benign, if unimaginative, media made my task easier. Ironically, political correctness is less obvious, though the life — and deification — of Eve van Grafhorst is a reminder that the media still finds it hard to see anyone other than children or haemophiliacs as innocents.

These jobs required me to assume a 'public relations' guise at times, but for a person who still regards himself as primarily a journalist, this was acceptable because HIV/ AIDS is a cause I believe in and it raises so many fascinating issues. Ironically, too, the gay environment of both the Trust and the Foundation was sometimes almost overpowering, so great a contrast was it to my schooling and teaching experiences.

Since Kevarnos, I've only had one major relationship: Ian, whom I met in London on (yes!) Valentine's Day. It was six months into this intense relationship that I received the job offer from the New Zealand AIDS Foundation — an opportunity to return 'home' which I decided to take. Ultimately, distance defeated us but, in the back of my mind, I believe, time would have anyway. Ian's a beautiful man but, when I met him, he had still to get over his last love. And he's since found a substitute for mine.

At time of writing I have yet to find the love I seek but find some solace through close friends and family. Nothing scares people off like desperation, and I am open to love, not chasing after it. Casual sex is fine — as far as it goes — but, who knows, by the time you read this, I may have found someone who is right for me.

My work and life experience thus far has taught me a few

valuable lessons. I no longer edit who I am to suit people's prejudices, and I see plenty of signs of positive change around me. Most gay people go through a phase of rationalising their sexuality, but after a while this ceases to be all-consuming. You get a life and you get to enjoy one of the best things in life: how beautiful men are, or can be. Why some people lack the imagination to understand this dynamic in a gay relationship remains a genuine mystery to me. One of the best things about being gay is being able to physically enjoy male beauty *and* the ideal. I appreciate female beauty in a different way, it is true, but I can respect the ideal and wonder why others remain so rigid in their views. Part of my wonderful journey so far in this life has been that, instead of seeing the gay community *en masse*, I've learnt to appreciate the individuals and experiences that define who and what we are, without making us uniform.